High Crimes and Misdemeanors
The Impeachment Process

CRIME, JUSTICE, AND PUNISHMENT

High Crimes and Misdemeanors
The Impeachment Process

Justin Fernandez

Austin Sarat, GENERAL EDITOR

CHELSEA HOUSE PUBLISHERS
Philadelphia

Frontispiece: *The House Judiciary Committee votes on an article of impeachment against President Clinton, December 12, 1998.*

Cover Photos: AP/WIDE WORLD PHOTOS

Chelsea House Publishers

Editor in Chief Stephen Reginald
Managing Editor James D. Gallagher
Production Manager Pamela Loos
Art Director Sara Davis
Director of Photography Judy L. Hasday
Senior Production Editor J. Christopher Higgins

Staff for HIGH CRIMES AND MISDEMEANORS

Senior Editor John Ziff
Associate Art Director Takeshi Takahashi
Designer Keith Trego
Picture Researcher Sandy Jones
Cover Designer Keith Trego

First Printing

1 3 5 7 9 8 6 4 2

The Chelsea House World Wide Web address is
http://www.chelseahouse.com

Library of Congress Cataloging-in-Publication Data applied for

ISBN 0-7910-5450-0

Contents

CRIME, JUSTICE, AND PUNISHMENT

Fears and Fascinations:

An Introduction to
Crime, Justice, and Punishment

By Austin Sarat

We live with crime and images of crime all around us. Crime evokes in most of us a deep aversion, a feeling of profound vulnerability, but it also evokes an equally deep fascination. Today, in major American cities the fear of crime is a major fact of life, some would say a disproportionate response to the realities of crime. Yet the fear of crime is real, palpable in the quickened steps and furtive glances of people walking down darkened streets. At the same time, we eagerly follow crime stories on television and in movies. We watch with a "who done it" curiosity, eager to see the illicit deed done, the investigation undertaken, the miscreant brought to justice and given his just deserts. On the streets the presence of crime is a reminder of our own vulnerability and the precariousness of our taken-for-granted rights and freedoms. On television and in the movies the crime story gives us a chance to probe our own darker motives, to ask "Is there a criminal within?" as well as to feel the collective satisfaction of seeing justice done.

Fear and fascination, these two poles of our engagement with crime, are, of course, only part of the story. Crime is, after all, a major social and legal problem, not just an issue of our individual psychology. Politicians today use our fear of, and fascination with, crime for political advantage. How we respond to crime, as well as to the political uses of the crime issue, tells us a lot about who we are as a people as well as what we value and what we tolerate. Is our response compassionate or severe? Do we seek to understand or to punish, to enact an angry vengeance or to rehabilitate and welcome the criminal back into our midst? The CRIME, JUSTICE, AND PUNISHMENT series is designed to explore these themes, to ask why we are fearful and fascinated, to probe the meanings and motivations of crimes and criminals and of our responses to them, and, finally, to ask what we can learn about ourselves and the society in which we live by examining our responses to crime.

Crime is always a challenge to the prevailing normative order and a test of the values and commitments of law-abiding people. It is sometimes a Raskolnikov-like act of defiance, an assertion of the unwillingness of some to live according to the rules of conduct laid out by organized society. In this sense, crime marks the limits of the law and reminds us of law's all-too-regular failures. Yet sometimes there is more desperation than defiance in criminal acts; sometimes they signal a deep pathology or need in the criminal. To confront crime is thus also to come face-to-face with the reality of social difference, of class privilege and extreme deprivation, of race and racism, of children neglected, abandoned, or abused whose response is to enact on others what they have experienced themselves. And occasionally crime, or what is labeled a criminal act, represents a call for justice, an appeal to a higher moral order against the inadequacies of existing law.

Figuring out the meaning of crime and the motivations of criminals and whether crime arises from defiance, desperation, or the appeal for justice is never an easy task. The motivations and meanings of crime are as varied as are the persons who engage in criminal conduct. They are as mysterious as any of the mysteries of the human soul. Yet the desire to know the secrets of crime and the criminal is a strong one, for in that knowledge may lie one step on the road to protection, if not an assurance of one's own personal safety. Nonetheless, as strong as that desire may be, there is no available technology that can allow us to know the whys of crime with much confidence, let alone a scientific certainty. We can, however, capture something about crime by studying the defiance, desperation, and quest for justice that may be associated with it. Books in the CRIME, JUSTICE, AND PUNISHMENT series will take up that challenge. They tell stories of crime and criminals, some famous, most not, some glamorous and exciting, most mundane and commonplace.

This series will, in addition, take a sober look at American criminal justice, at the procedures through which we investigate crimes and identify criminals, at the institutions in which innocence or guilt is determined. In these procedures and institutions we confront the thrill of the chase as well as the challenge of protecting the rights of those who defy our laws. It is through the efficiency and dedication of law enforcement that we might capture the criminal; it is in the rare instances of their corruption or brutality that we feel perhaps our deepest betrayal. Police, prosecutors, defense lawyers, judges, and jurors administer criminal justice and in their daily actions give substance to the guarantees of the Bill of Rights. What is an adversarial system of justice? How does it work? Why do we have it? Books in the CRIME, JUSTICE, AND PUNISHMENT series will examine the thrill of the chase as we seek to capture the criminal. They will also reveal the drama and majesty of the criminal trial as well as the day-to-day reality of a criminal justice system in which trials are the exception and negotiated pleas of guilty are the rule.

When the trial is over or the plea has been entered, when we have separated the innocent from the guilty, the moment of punishment has arrived. The injunction to punish the guilty, to respond to pain inflicted by inflicting pain, is as old as civilization itself. "An eye for an eye and a tooth for a tooth" is a biblical reminder that punishment must measure pain for pain. But our response to the criminal must be better than and different from the crime itself. The biblical admonition, along with the constitutional prohibition of "cruel and unusual punishment," signals that we seek to punish justly and to be just not only in the determination of who can and should be punished, but in how we punish as well. But neither reminder tells us what to do with the wrongdoer. Do we rape the rapist, or burn the home of the arsonist? Surely justice and decency say no. But, if not, then how can and should we punish? In a world in which punishment is neither identical to the crime nor an automatic response to it, choices must be made and we must make them. Books in the Crime, Justice, and Punishment series will examine those choices and the practices, and politics, of punishment. How do we punish and why do we punish as we do? What can we learn about the rationality and appropriateness of today's responses to crime by examining our past and its responses? What works? Is there, and can there be, a just measure of pain?

CRIME, JUSTICE, AND PUNISHMENT brings together books on some of the great themes of human social life. The books in this series capture our fear and fascination with crime and examine our responses to it. They remind us of the deadly seriousness of these subjects. They bring together themes in law, literature, and popular culture to challenge us to think again, to think anew, about subjects that go to the heart of who we are and how we can and will live together.

*   *   *   *   *

Impeachment is a rare, but also an important, event. It is a moment when politics is infused with a juridical spirit, and when law is inevitably cast in partisan terms. This was surely one of the important lessons of the recent impeachment of President Clinton. In that case and in others, impeachment represents the commitment of our constitutional order to ensuring both continuity and accountability in our highest public offices. In the case of the impeachment of a president, the procedure is a way of undoing the democratic decision of a national election. When it is applied to judges, impeachment helps to ensure that life tenure does not turn to caprice.

In this timely book, Justin Fernandez provides a comprehensive treatment of a subject that is not well understood. Starting with the case against President Clinton, he provides the historical and political background of the impeachment process that is necessary to help us make sense of that most dramatic of recent events. Taking us back to the Constitutional Convention, this book provides a helpful sense of what those who authored the Constitution meant by the phrase "high crimes and misdemeanors." This historically rooted but elusive phrase was and is the touchstone for impeachment. Moreover, by comparing presidential and judicial impeachment, Fernandez reminds us not only of the grandeur of the impeachment process, but also of its potential for abuse. Filled with gripping examples of the use of the impeachment process as well as a sophisticated sense of its complications, *High Crimes and Misdemeanors* shows all the ways that impeachment puts our constitutional system to one of its most severe tests.

"That Is Absolutely True"

On May 6, 1994, Paula Corbin Jones filed a federal civil rights lawsuit. The suit would have been unremarkable except for the identity of one of its defendants: William Jefferson Clinton, 42nd president of the United States.

Jones, a former Arkansas state employee, alleged that while Clinton was governor of Arkansas—and hence her boss—he sexually harassed her. Jones claimed that during a state development conference at the Excelsior Hotel in Little Rock, Arkansas, on May 8, 1991, Clinton arranged a meeting with her in one of the hotel rooms. Once the two were alone, Jones alleged, he complimented her on her looks, kissed her, lowered his trousers and underwear, and invited her to perform oral sex.

As with many sexual harassment cases, the alleged behavior had occurred in private, with no eyewitnesses other than the two opposing parties in the lawsuit. Thus, like most cases of alleged sexual harassment, the

William Jefferson Clinton, 42nd president of the United States and defendant in a sexual harassment lawsuit.

Paula Corbin Jones and her husband, Stephen, arrive at the Washington law offices of President Clinton's private attorney, Robert Bennett. In 1994 Jones filed a lawsuit alleging that three years earlier, while he was governor of Arkansas, Clinton had propositioned her in a hotel room in Little Rock.

Jones lawsuit would boil down to a credibility battle. Jones's chances of winning would depend largely upon her lawyers' ability to show a pattern of similar misconduct by Clinton. As the Equal Employment Opportunity Commission explained in a 1990 policy statement, a plaintiff's allegations of an incident of sexual harassment "would be further buttressed if other employees testified that the supervisor propositioned them as well." Such corroboration can show the defendant's "motive, opportunity, intent, preparation, plan, knowledge, identity, or absence of mistake or accident." The way Jones's lawyers would learn about other occasions when Clinton had acted inappropriately—if such occasions existed—was through the legal process of discovery.

Generally the purpose of discovery in a civil lawsuit is to allow a wide-ranging search for facts, the names of witnesses, and evidence that may aid a party in the preparation or presentation of his or her case. The discovery process enables the parties to obtain from their respective opponents, under oath, written answers to written questions and oral testimony in depositions (out-of-court legal proceedings involving the questioning of a witness under oath), along with documents and other tangible items that could be of use later in presenting the case. There are limits to what may be requested in pretrial discovery, however: the information sought must appear reasonably calculated to lead to the discovery of admissible evidence. In other words, discovery cannot be used merely to embarrass or harass a legal opponent.

In an order dated December 11, 1997, the federal judge hearing the Jones lawsuit, Judge Susan Webber Wright, ruled that Jones was "entitled to information regarding any individuals with whom the President had sexual relations or proposed or sought to have sexual relations and who were during the relevant time frame state or federal employees."

In mid-December 1997, the president answered one of the written discovery questions posed by Jones's lawyers on this issue. When asked under oath to identify all women who were state or federal employees and with whom he had engaged in "sexual relations" (the term was not explicitly defined) since 1986, the president answered: "None."

As discovery proceeded in the Paula Jones sexual harassment lawsuit, another legal investigation of the president was also moving along. Though wide-ranging, this investigation as yet had nothing to do with sex. Like the Jones case, however, its origins lay in events that had occurred while Bill Clinton was a prominent political figure in Arkansas.

In 1978 Clinton, then the attorney general of

Arkansas, and his wife, Hillary, became partners in a land development project with their friends Susan and James McDougal. The four bought 220 acres in the Ozark Mountains, hoping to develop the property into vacation homes under the name Whitewater Development Corporation. Four years later James McDougal purchased Madison Guaranty, a Little Rock savings and loan. Over the next decade Madison, the Whitewater Development Corporation, the McDougals, the Clintons, and several other friends would be involved in a confusing tangle of land deals, loans, and legal work done by Hillary Clinton's law firm. According to federal bank examiners, at least one project, the Castle Grande deal, was completely fraudulent.

Rumors of illegality in Whitewater-related dealings—by the Clintons and their associates—circulated during the 1992 presidential campaign. But it was not until 1994, when Clinton was in the second year of his presidency, that a full-scale investigation began. That investigation was conducted by the Office of Independent Counsel (OIC).

Situations like the Whitewater matter were what Congress had in mind when it passed the Independent Counsel Act of 1978, which created the OIC. Typically, the Justice Department investigates allegations of criminal wrongdoing in the federal government. But because the attorney general—the head of the Justice Department—is a political appointee of the president, concerns might arise regarding the independence of such an investigation when the targets are high-ranking members of the executive branch. Might a president be able to influence an investigation, to shield himself or his associates? Indeed, that is precisely what President Richard Nixon had tried to do in 1974, in the midst of the Watergate scandal. To ensure fairness and avoid even the appearance of favoritism or a conflict of interest, the Independent Counsel Act required the attorney general to seek the appointment of an

Monica Lewinsky was a young White House intern when she and Bill Clinton became involved in a sexual relationship. Efforts to conceal that relationship during the Jones lawsuit would ultimately lead to the president's impeachment.

outside investigator, called an independent counsel, when substantial evidence existed of wrongdoing by the president or members of his cabinet.

In January 1994, Attorney General Janet Reno recommended that the Special Division of the United States Court of Appeals for the District of Columbia Circuit—a three-judge panel charged with appointing independent counsels—choose lawyer Robert Fiske as independent counsel to investigate Whitewater. Fiske, a prominent Republican, began his investigation of the Democratic president and his associates by convening a grand jury—a jury assembled to hear evidence and decide whether to indict, or charge, a defendant—in Little Rock. After little more than six months, however, powerful Republicans in Congress complained that Fiske was not being aggressive enough, and the Special Division replaced him with another prominent Republican, former federal judge Kenneth Starr.

Over the next three and a half years, Starr and his OIC lawyers and investigators would probe not just the Whitewater affair—the original reason for the appointment of the independent counsel—but also a variety of other matters: the firing of the White House Travel Office staff; the suicide of Vincent Foster, deputy White House counsel and a close friend of the Clintons; and the discovery of confidential FBI files at the White House. The statute creating the OIC gave independent counsels broad latitude and unlimited time and resources to conduct their inquiries.

In January 1997, as Starr and his team continued investigating Whitewater and other matters, Paula Jones's attorney received information that could be pertinent to Jones's sexual-harassment lawsuit: a story was circulating that in November 1993 the president had groped and propositioned a former White House volunteer named Kathleen Willey.

In October of the same year, Jones's new legal team received information that was potentially even more explosive: a former White House intern, Monica Lewinsky, had told another former White House employee, Linda Tripp, about a sexual affair she had had with President Clinton. In fact, Tripp had tape-recorded numerous phone conversations with Lewinsky, during which the two had discussed the affair.

On January 12, 1998, the two investigations of President Clinton—by the lawyers for Paula Jones and

by the OIC—would converge. On that day Linda Tripp contacted the OIC, revealing that she had information that one of the witnesses in the Jones case—Lewinsky—was prepared to provide false testimony under oath about her relationship with President Clinton and was attempting to get Tripp to lie as well.

Asking someone to lie under oath is called suborning perjury (perjury being the actual lie while under oath), and it is a federal crime. Tripp turned over some of the tapes of her conversations with Lewinsky. On one of those tapes, Lewinsky was indeed heard asking Tripp to lie under oath about Lewinsky's affair with the president. The OIC was also informed that Lewinsky had spoken to the president and to his close friend and confidant, Washington lawyer Vernon Jordan, about being subpoenaed to testify in the Jones suit, and that Vernon Jordan and others were helping Lewinsky find employment to

Linda Tripp secretly taped phone conversations with her friend Monica Lewinsky during which the two discussed Lewinsky's relationship with President Clinton. Tripp shared her story with both the Office of Independent Counsel, which was investigating the president on unrelated matters, and Paula Jones's attorneys.

keep her quiet about the affair.

Armed with this new information, Starr requested permission from the attorney general to expand the four-year-old OIC investigation yet again, to include matters related to the Paula Jones sexual harassment lawsuit. The request was not unprecedented: other independent counsels had broadened the scope of their original investigations as they uncovered information. In addition, Starr's request made a certain amount of sense from a practical standpoint. If Attorney General Reno were to recommend that a different independent counsel be appointed to investigate Tripp's charges, that person would have to start from square one, assembling an investigative and legal staff. Starr already had a staff in place and could theoretically conduct a timely and cost-effective probe.

What Starr did not tell Reno was that he had a minor connection to Paula Jones's legal effort: earlier he had been asked to advise on the constitutionality of suing a sitting president. Critics would later take Starr to task for this omission, claiming that Reno would not have allowed him to expand his probe had she known of the connection. In any event, in the absence of knowledge about Starr's earlier legal advice, Reno petitioned the Special Division, on an expedited basis, to expand the jurisdiction of Independent Counsel Kenneth W. Starr.

On January 16, 1998, in response to the attorney general's request, the Special Division issued an order that provided in pertinent part:

> The Independent Counsel shall have jurisdiction and authority to investigate to the maximum extent authorized by the Independent Counsel Reauthorization Act of 1994 whether Monica Lewinsky or others suborned perjury, obstructed justice, intimidated witnesses, or otherwise violated federal law other than a Class B or C misdemeanor or infraction in dealing with witnesses, potential witnesses, attorneys, or others concerning the civil case *Jones v. Clinton*.

On January 14, Lewinsky had handed Tripp a typed, three-page document entitled "Points to Make in an Affidavit." (An affidavit is a sworn statement of truth.) Among other things the memo asked Tripp, as a witness in the Jones case, to declare that Monica Lewinsky was a "huge liar" and had been "stalking" the president "or something like that." This would have the effect of casting doubt on any statements Lewinsky had made about her relationship with Clinton. The memo also suggested that Tripp submit her affidavit to the president's legal team for review.

Lewinsky herself had already submitted an affidavit in the Jones case denying any sexual affair with the president. The president's lawyer, Robert Bennett, was about to use this affidavit in questioning Clinton during a deposition.

At the beginning of that deposition the president took an oath administered by Judge Wright: "Do you swear or affirm . . . that the testimony you are about to give in the matter before the court is the truth, the whole truth, and nothing but the truth, so help you God?"

The president replied: "I do."

Before questioning the president, Jones's attorneys asked: "And your testimony is subject to the penalty of perjury; do you understand that, sir?"

The president responded: "I do."

Jones's attorneys then asked the president specific questions about possible sexual activity with Monica Lewinsky. (They were aware of Lewinsky's relationship with Clinton because Linda Tripp had briefed them—after contacting the OIC—about the existence and content of her taped conversations with Lewinsky.) The attorneys used various terms in their queries, including

Judge Susan Webber Wright presided over the case of Jones v. Clinton.

"sexual affair," "sexual relationship," and "sexual rela-tions." However, "sexual affair" and "sexual relation-ship" were not specifically defined by Jones's attorneys. The term "sexual relations" was defined as follows:

> For the purposes of this deposition, a person engages in "sexual relations" when the person knowingly engages in or causes . . . contact with the genitalia, anus, groin, breast, inner thigh, or buttocks of any person with an intent to arouse or gratify the sexual desire of any person. . . . "Contact" means intentional touching, either directly or through clothing.

President Clinton then answered a series of ques-tions about his relationship with Lewinsky, including:

> Q: Did you have an extramarital sexual affair with Mon-ica Lewinsky?
>
> President Clinton: No.
>
> Q: If she told someone that she had a sexual affair with you beginning in November of 1995, would that be a lie?
>
> President Clinton: It's certainly not the truth. It would not be the truth.
>
> Q: I think I used the term "sexual affair." And so the record is completely clear, have you ever had sexual rela-tions with Monica Lewinsky, as that term is defined in Deposition Exhibit 1, as modified by the Court?
>
> Mr. Bennett: I object because I don't know that he can remember—
>
> Judge Wright: Well, it's real short. He can—I will permit the question and you may show the witness definition number one.
>
> President Clinton: I have never had sexual relations with Monica Lewinsky. I've never had an affair with her.

During the deposition, the president's attorney also sought to limit questioning about Lewinsky. Bennett told Judge Wright that Lewinsky executed "an affidavit which [Jones's lawyers] are in possession of saying that there is absolutely no sex of any kind in any manner, shape or form, with President Clinton." In a subsequent colloquy (question-and-answer discussion) with Judge Wright, Bennett declared that as a result of "preparation of [President Clinton] for this deposition, the witness is fully aware of Ms. Lewinsky's affidavit."

Clinton did not dispute his lawyer's assertion that the president and Lewinsky had engaged in "absolutely no sex of any kind in any manner, shape or form." Nor did Clinton dispute the implication that Lewinsky's affidavit, in denying "a sexual relationship," meant that there was "absolutely no sex of any kind in any manner, shape or form."

In subsequent questioning by his attorney, President Clinton testified under oath as follows:

> Q: In paragraph eight of [Lewinsky's] affidavit, she says this: "I have never had a sexual relationship with the President, he did not propose that we have a sexual relationship, he did not offer me employment or other benefits in exchange for a sexual relationship, he did not deny me employment or other benefits for rejecting a sexual relationship." Is that a true and accurate statement as far as you know it?
>
> President Clinton: That is absolutely true.

"SHALL ANY MAN BE ABOVE JUSTICE?"

"Shall any man be above justice?" George Mason pauses, his voice echoing in the State House, the old Independence Hall in Philadelphia. He looks at the crowd. George Washington, Benjamin Franklin, Alexander Hamilton, and many other heroes of the American Revolution—the so-called Founding Fathers—return his gaze, listening intently while Mason, an original signer of the Declaration of Independence, argues in favor of allowing a sitting president to be impeached.

It is the summer of 1787, and the first Constitutional Convention is deciding how the new republic, the United States of America, is going to be governed. Colonel Mason, one of the delegates to the conven-

George Washington addresses the delegates to the Constitutional Convention, 1787. As they worked to craft a document creating a stable but not overly powerful federal government, the Founding Fathers had to confront the problem of what to do when a president was accused of wrongdoing.

tion, is helping to frame the language of the Constitution. The delegates will thus come to be known as the Framers of the Constitution.

George Washington, who in 1789 will become the first president elected by the people, spends the entire summer at the Constitutional Convention. Washington is so popular that historians will credit his presence alone with keeping the delegates together long enough to finally reach agreement. Later, Washington's support and approval of the final form of the Constitution will influence the ratification (official approval) of the Constitution by the legislatures of the 13 states.

James Madison, who will be elected president of the United States some 21 years hence, takes notes during the many days of debates. Among the issues is how to remove an elected or appointed official who has abused government power.

It is clear to most of the delegates that this removal power, consisting of charges (impeachment) and a trial (an impeachment trial) is a most important feature of this plan. Without impeachment, the people could not hold appointed or elected officials accountable for their behavior. But crafting a system preventing impeachment for purely political motives while ensuring a fair process for, as Madison is to write, "defending the community against the incapacity, negligence, or perfidy of the Chief Executive" is proving to be a difficult problem.

The Framers expect politics, like human nature, to change very little in the future. They foresee opposing political parties fighting over the merits of most, if not all, impeachments, and most often exhibiting partisanship, or party loyalty, instead of more objective, impartial judgment.

Such partisanship causes spirited debate at the Constitutional Convention. The Framers are divided mostly into two parties: Federalists, who support the idea of a stronger central government, and Anti-Federalists, who are concerned about oppression from

Massachusetts delegate Elbridge Gerry urged his fellow conventioneers not to assume that a president could do no wrong.

a too-powerful federal government.

Colonel Mason is appalled that anyone could oppose the idea of impeaching a president during his term in office. "No point is of more importance than that the right of impeachment should be continued," he argues. "Shall any man be above Justice? Above all shall that man be above it, who can commit the most extensive injustice?"

But Congressman Charles Pinckney of South Carolina, a 29-year-old attorney, immediately objects to Mason's advocacy of in-term impeachments. Pinckney agrees with the practice of Virginia and Delaware, where executive impeachments must be delayed until after the executive's departure from office.

North Carolina delegate William R. Davie counters. If the president is not impeachable while in office,

Davie says, then an essential security for the good behavior of the chief executive will be lost.

Delegate Benjamin Franklin, now 81 years old and president of Pennsylvania, supports the idea that the Constitution allow for the executive's removal if his misconduct deserves it, and for "his honorable acquittal should the accusation prove unjust." Franklin, who despite declining health is active at the Constitutional Convention, has his speeches read for him by Scottish-born James Wilson, a signer of the Declaration of Independence, a future associate justice of the United States Supreme Court, and a fellow Pennsylvania delegate.

Before Wilson reads Dr. Franklin's opinion on impeachments, Massachusetts delegate Elbridge Gerry speaks. Gerry, who will later serve a two-year stint as vice president in James Madison's administration, begins arguing that a legitimate basis for impeachment is "malpractice or neglect of duty."

Pennsylvania delegate Gouverneur Morris, a 33-year-old lawyer, merchant, and financier—a man who has called the slave trade a "nefarious institution" in his bid to have the delegates adopt an explicitly worded constitutional prohibition of slavery—admits his belief that corruption and "some few other offenses" should be impeachable. But Morris wants each impeachable offense listed and defined.

Pinckney disagrees again. He says that a legislature's power to threaten the president with impeachment in order to obtain legislative advantage threatens the independence of the executive.

Gerry then appeals to the delegates' sensibilities, saying that he hopes they will not adopt the maxim that the president could do no wrong. Gerry reminds his fellow conventioneers that a good magistrate will not fear a threat of impeachment.

Rufus King, 32 years old and a businessman and member of the Massachusetts Legislature, notes that judges serve for a term of "good behavior," and there-

fore impeachment is proper for them. A president serving during elective tenure, on the other hand, should
not be impeachable by the legislature. King continues,
saying, "I rely on the vigor of the Executive as a great
security for the public liberties." He adds that impeachment by the legislature will destroy the "primitive
axiom that the three great departments of Government
[the executive, legislative, and judicial branches]
should be separate and independent."

After King finishes, 34-year-old Virginia delegate
Edmund Randolph speaks. Randolph, one of the
framers of the first Constitution of Virginia, urges sim-
ply and powerfully that "guilt wherever found ought to
be punished."

"MOST ORDINARY AMERICANS"

In the space of a single day, January 21, 1998, the OIC investigation of President Clinton exploded into a national obsession. The Whitewater matter had been confusing and difficult to characterize even for Washington pundits, and the investigation had for the most part failed to capture the attention of ordinary Americans. But now, in an article posted early in the morning on its Web page, the *Washington Post* was reporting that Independent Counsel Kenneth Starr had won approval to expand his investigation again—into allegations the president had a sexual affair with former White House intern Monica Lewinsky and tried to get her to lie about it under oath in the Jones lawsuit.

By evening the story was dominating the airwaves, and millions of Americans had heard some stunning

Breaking news: White House press secretary Mike McCurry fields reporters' questions on January 21, 1998, the day news of the president's possible affair with Monica Lewinsky became public.

31

details: Another former White House employee, Linda Tripp, had tape-recorded conversations with Lewinsky during which the two had discussed in graphic language Lewinsky's alleged affair with the president. Tripp also claimed to have heard phone messages the president left on Lewinsky's answering machine. Starr's office had wired Tripp to secretly record Lewinsky during a lunch.

When Clinton kept a previously scheduled commitment to appear on the PBS news program *The NewsHour with Jim Lehrer* that night, the Lewinsky matter was the first subject that came up. Clinton denied suborning Lewinsky to commit perjury. On the question of whether he had had an affair with the intern, he stated, "There is no improper relationship."

"No improper relationship. Define what you mean by that," Lehrer asked.

"I think you know what it means," Clinton responded. "It means there is not a sexual relationship, an improper sexual relationship, or any other kind of improper relationship."

Lehrer followed up. "You had no sexual relationship with this young woman?"

"There is not a sexual relationship. That is accurate," Clinton answered.

More than one commentator noted the president's apparently careful use of the present tense.

In California, Clinton's good friend Harry Thomason, a Hollywood producer who had occasionally advised the president on matters relating to the media, saw the interview and thought that Clinton had come off weakly. Thomason traveled to Washington, D.C., the following day and met with the president. According to later accounts of the meeting developed by Kenneth Starr's investigators, Thomason recommended that Clinton "should explain it so there's no doubt in anybody's mind that nothing happened." The president agreed. "You know, you're right. I should be more force-

ful than that," he is reported to have said.

On January 23, President Clinton started a cabinet meeting by saying the allegations were untrue. Afterward, several cabinet members appeared before reporters gathered outside the White House. Secretary of State Madeleine Albright said, "I believe that the allegations are completely untrue." "I'll second that, definitely," Commerce Secretary William Daley said. Secretary of Education Richard Riley and Secretary of Health and Human Services Donna Shalala concurred.

The next day, Ann Lewis, White House communications director, publicly announced that "those of us who have wanted to go out and speak on behalf of the president" had been given the green light by the president's legal team. Lewis reported that the president answered the allegations "directly" by denying any

After the Lewinsky story broke, the news media found—and repeatedly showed—this video image of the president hugging the intern at a 1996 White House lawn party.

President Clinton's personal secretary, Betty Currie, and his longtime friend Vernon Jordan were key to the OIC investigation into possible obstruction of justice.

improper relationship. She believed that, in issuing his public denials, the president was not "splitting hairs, defining what is a sexual relationship, talking about 'is' rather than was."

On Monday, January 26, 1998, President Clinton spoke for himself. At an event promoting after-school health care, the president denied the allegations in the strongest terms. "I want to say one thing to the American people," Clinton declared. "I want you to listen to me. I'm not going to say this again: I did not have sexual relations with that woman, Miss Lewinsky. I never told anybody to lie, not a single time. Never. These allegations are false." This would turn out to be the president's last public statement for several months on the Lewinsky matter.

In the meantime, the president won a legal victory in the case from which the Lewinsky matter had arisen. On April 1, 1998, Judge Susan Webber Wright dismissed Paula Jones's sexual harassment lawsuit, concluding that even if the facts Jones alleged were true, her claims failed as a matter of law. Jones had not demonstrated any negative consequences, such as loss of employment or failure to win promotions, as the result of her rebuffing Clinton's alleged proposition.

Many Clinton supporters believed that the Lewinsky matter would disappear with Judge Wright's decision. But the dismissal of the Jones case did not affect Starr's criminal investigation of the president. The inquiry continued, the OIC maintained, because of the seriousness of "any attempt to obstruct the proper functioning of the judicial system, regardless of the perceived merits of the underlying [Jones] case."

In Washington, Starr had impaneled a federal grand jury. He subpoenaed dozens of witnesses to appear before the grand jury and be questioned by OIC prosecutors. Four witnesses became central to the OIC's case.

Betty Currie, the president's secretary, was an important witness because she knew of Lewinsky's frequent visits to the Oval Office. In addition, Currie was at the center of what prosecutors saw as an instance of obstruction of justice. In December 1997, as discovery was proceeding in the Paula Jones case, Currie took possession of gifts that Clinton had given Lewinsky. By order of the court, such gifts were to have been turned over as evidence in the Jones lawsuit. The question was, had Currie retrieved the gifts at Clinton's behest? Or had it been Monica Lewinsky's idea to return the gifts to the president's secretary, as Currie would recall? Currie had also had a rather curious conversation with the president right after his deposition in the Jones case. Clinton, by his own later admission, had been surprised at the specificity of the questions Jones's lawyers

For months the question of what Monica Lewinsky might say about her relationship with President Clinton remained a matter of intense speculation. Finally, lawyers for Lewinsky and the OIC hammered out an immunity agreement, and the former intern testified before Kenneth Starr's grand jury.

had posed about his relationship with Monica Lewinsky. He now asked Currie a series of questions that sounded more like statements: "You were always there when [Lewinsky] was there, right? We were never really alone." "Monica came on to me and I never touched her, right?" Prosecutors saw this as an attempt to influence the testimony of a possible witness in the case, although Currie would testify that she didn't feel pressured to agree with the president and Clinton would claim, somewhat improbably, that he was trying to refresh his memory on the facts.

Washington lawyer Vernon Jordan, a close friend

of the president, was key to the OIC's case primarily because Jordan had helped Monica Lewinsky look for a job. Jordan, who sat on the board of directors of Revlon, had placed calls on Lewinsky's behalf to several business leaders he knew. When Lewinsky interviewed with MacAndrews & Forbes Holdings (MFH)—the corporate owner of Revlon—but failed to receive a job offer, Jordan even called the chairman and chief financial officer of MFH to personally recommend Lewinsky. Prosecutors maintained that Jordan's effort amounted to what is called a quid pro quo arrangement—in exchange for Jordan's help finding a job, Lewinsky would remain silent about her affair with the president. But in front of the grand jury, Jordan testified that he hadn't known of the sexual relationship between Lewinsky and the president. In addition, the job search had been initiated in mid-October 1997, and Lewinsky and Jordan had first met on November 5. It wasn't until December 5 that Lewinsky was first listed as a potential witness in the Jones case.

Lewinsky herself became the OIC's star witness, but only after an agreement protecting her from prosecution had been hammered out after months of negotiations. Starr's prosecutors had first confronted Lewinsky on January 16, 1998, threatening her with criminal charges if she didn't immediately cooperate with their investigation. However, it wasn't until July that Lewinsky did start cooperating in exchange for immunity.

On August 6 she began her testimony before the grand jury. Lewinsky testified that, beginning in November 1995, when she was a 22-year-old White House intern, she had a relationship with the president that included substantial sexual activity. According to Lewinsky, such activity had included kissing, fondling, and oral sex performed by her on the president, but not sexual intercourse. She testified in detail about the times, dates, and nature of 10 sexual encounters that involved some form of genital contact. White House records mostly corroborated this aspect of Lewinsky's testimony; the president was in the Oval Office area during the encounters, and while the records of White House entry and exit are incomplete for employees, they do show Lewinsky's presence in the White House on eight of the occasions in question.

As for the obstruction of justice allegations, Lewinsky maintained that no one had asked her to lie, nor had she been promised a job in exchange for her silence. Starr's prosecutors would argue, however, that Lewinsky didn't need to be told explicitly to lie because she and Clinton had long before worked out "cover stories" to conceal their relationship.

If Monica Lewinsky was a hugely important grand jury witness, the biggest witness of all was President Clinton himself. The OIC had subpoenaed the president but, in the face of a promised legal battle, had later withdrawn the subpoena after the two parties agreed on special conditions for Clinton's testimony. Unlike other witnesses, who had to appear at the courthouse where the grand jury met, the president would be questioned by Starr's lawyers at the White House. The testimony would be transmitted in real time to the courtroom so the grand jurors could see it. The session would also be videotaped, according to the OIC because one grand juror could not be present. Unlike other grand jury witnesses, Clinton would be permitted to have his lawyer in the room during testimony, and perhaps most significantly, the session would be limited to four hours.

By the time Clinton testified on August 17, 1998, the president couldn't plausibly deny that sexual activity had occurred between him and Monica Lewinsky. Her grand jury testimony to the contrary was on the record, but more importantly, there was incontrovertible physical evidence: forensic tests had revealed the presence of semen on a blue dress owned by Lewinsky, and further DNA tests had established

that the semen was Clinton's.

In his videotaped grand jury testimony, the president attempted to walk a fine line. While now acknowledging "inappropriate intimate contact" with Lewinsky, he maintained that his January deposition in the Jones case had been technically truthful. "I wanted to be legal without being particularly helpful," Clinton said, explaining that he didn't believe it had been his responsibility to do the work of Jones's lawyers for them—especially because their whole purpose, in his view, was to embarrass and damage him politically.

At times the defense he now offered relied on an extremely literal interpretation of words. For example, during the Jones deposition the president's attorney, Robert Bennett, had objected to certain questions about

President Clinton makes a point during his videotaped grand jury testimony. In his hand is a copy of the definition of sexual relations that was used during his deposition in the Jones lawsuit. The president's insistence that he had been technically truthful during that deposition led to an impeachment charge.

Monica Lewinsky, saying, "Counsel [for Paula Jones] is fully aware that Ms. Lewinsky has filed . . . an affidavit, which they are in possession of, saying that there is absolutely no sex of any kind in any manner, shape or form with President Clinton." When Starr's prosecutors challenged Clinton to explain why he had not corrected that assertion, which he knew to be untrue, Clinton responded, "Well, actually, in the present tense, that's an accurate statement. . . . that was an accurate statement." His reasoning: at the time of the deposition, there was no sex of any kind between him and Lewinsky because they had discontinued their physical relationship months before. When pressed later in his grand jury testimony to admit that saying that Bennett's words

11 Possible Grounds for Impeachment, According to the Starr Report

1. President Clinton lied under oath in his civil case when he denied a sexual affair, a sexual relationship, or sexual relations with Monica Lewinsky.
2. President Clinton lied under oath to the grand jury about his sexual relationship with Ms. Lewinsky.
3. In his civil deposition, to support his false statement about the sexual relationship, President Clinton also lied under oath about being alone with Ms. Lewinsky and about the many gifts exchanged between Ms. Lewinsky and him.
4. President Clinton lied under oath in his civil deposition about his discussions with Ms. Lewinsky concerning her involvement in the Jones case.
5. During the Jones case, the President obstructed justice and had an understanding with Ms. Lewinsky to jointly conceal the truth about their relationship by concealing gifts subpoenaed by Ms. Jones's attorneys.
6. During the Jones case, the President obstructed justice and had an understanding with Ms. Lewinsky to jointly conceal the truth of their relationship from the judicial process by a scheme that included the following means: (i) Both the President and Ms. Lewinsky understood that they would lie under oath in the Jones case about their sexual relationship; (ii) the President suggested to Ms. Lewinsky that she prepare an affidavit that, for the President's purposes, would memorialize her testimony under oath and could be used to prevent questioning of both of them about their relationship; (iii) Ms. Lewinsky signed and filed the false affidavit; (iv) the President used Ms. Lewinsky's false affidavit at his deposition in an attempt to head off questions about Ms.

were accurate was "a completely false statement," Clinton stood firm. "It depends on what the meaning of the word 'is' means," he testified. "If 'is' means is, and never has been, that's one thing. If it means, there *is* none, that was a completely true statement."

Throughout the four hours of his grand jury testimony, the president steadfastly refused to answer specific questions about what physical acts he and Lewinsky had engaged in. He maintained that such questions were irrelevant to the core issue—whether he had committed perjury in denying a sexual relationship, sexual affair, or sexual relations with Lewinsky. The president insisted that all those terms— which were left undefined during the Jones deposition—require sexual intercourse,

Lewinsky; and (v) when that failed, the President lied under oath at his civil deposition about the relationship with Ms. Lewinsky.

7. President Clinton endeavored to obstruct justice by helping Ms. Lewinsky obtain a job in New York at a time when she would have been a witness harmful to him were she to tell the truth in the Jones case.
8. President Clinton lied under oath in his civil deposition about his discussions with Vernon Jordan concerning Ms. Lewinsky's involvement in the Jones case.
9. The President improperly tampered with a potential witness by attempting to corruptly influence the testimony of his personal secretary, Betty Currie, in the days after his civil deposition.
10. President Clinton endeavored to obstruct justice during the grand jury investigation by refusing to testify for seven months and lying to senior White House aides with knowledge that they would relay the President's false statements to the grand jury—and did thereby deceive, obstruct, and impede the grand jury.
11. President Clinton abused his constitutional authority by (i) lying to the public and the Congress in January 1998 about his relationship with Ms. Lewinsky; (ii) promising at that time to cooperate fully with the grand jury investigation; (iii) later refusing six invitations to testify voluntarily to the grand jury; (iv) invoking Executive Privilege; (v) lying to the grand jury in August 1998; and (vi) lying again to the public and Congress on August 17, 1998—all as part of an effort to hinder, impede, and deflect possible inquiry by the Congress of the United States.

regardless of what other acts may be involved. He stated that "most ordinary Americans" would embrace this distinction. Since he and Lewinsky had never had sexual intercourse, Clinton said, his testimony had not been perjurious.

Of course, a more specific definition of "sexual relations" had also been used at the civil deposition. That definition had stated that a person engages in "sexual relations" if he or she intentionally touches "the genitalia, anus, groin, breast, inner thigh, or buttocks of any person with an intent to arouse or gratify the sexual desire of any person." When asked whether Monica Lewinsky had performed oral sex on him, the president refused to say. But he did tell the grand jury that he didn't believe oral sex was covered by the definition as he understood it.

According to the president, the definition "covers contact by the person being deposed with the enumerated areas, if the contact is done with an intent to arouse or gratify," but it does not cover oral sex performed on the person being deposed: "[I]f the deponent is the person who has oral sex performed on him, then the contact is with—not with anything on that list, but with the lips of another person. It seems to be self-evident that that's what it is." In the president's view, "any person, reasonable person" would recognize that oral sex performed on the deponent falls outside the definition. Under this interpretation, had Lewinsky performed oral sex on the president, she would have engaged in sexual relations but the president would not.

The president did concede that contact with Lewinsky's breasts and genitalia would fall within the Jones definition of sexual relations. However, he denied that he had made such contact:

Q: The question is, if Monica Lewinsky says that while you were in the Oval Office area you touched her breasts would she be lying?

Independent Counsel Kenneth Starr.

President Clinton: That is not my recollection. My recollection is that I did not have sexual relations with Ms. Lewinsky and I'm staying on my former statement about that. . . . My—my statement is that I did not have sexual relations as defined by that.

Following his grand jury testimony, the president took his case to the American people in a brief televised address to the nation. Acknowledging that he had "misled people," Clinton admitted, "Indeed, I did have a relationship with Miss Lewinsky that was not appropriate. In fact, it was wrong." However, the president insisted that his testimony in the Jones deposition was "legally accurate" and that "at no time did I ask anyone to lie, to hide or destroy evidence or to take any other unlawful action."

And Clinton assailed what he viewed as politically motivated attempts to criminalize his private life. "I intend to reclaim my family life for my family," he declared. "It's nobody's business but ours. Even presidents have private lives. It is time to stop the pursuit of personal destruction and the prying into private lives and get on with our national life."

Others at the time also argued that alleged "lies about sex" had nothing to do with the president's performance in office, and so were inconsequential to any investigation of criminal or impeachable acts. Former White House counsel Jack Quinn articulated this view in saying, "This is a matter of sex between consenting adults, and the question of whether or not one or the other was truthful about it. . . . This doesn't go to the question of his conduct in office. And, in that sense, it's trivial."

In the days and weeks that followed, Americans of all political persuasions would debate whether the alleged conduct was "trivial" or whether it rose to the level of "high crimes and misdemeanors" and thus called for Clinton's removal from office. On September 9, 1998, the OIC weighed in on the matter with the submission to the House of Representatives of a referral—"substantial and credible information" that President Clinton "committed acts that may constitute grounds for impeachment." The lengthy document, which became known as the Starr Report, listed 11 possible grounds for impeachment related to obstruction of justice and perjury.

It would now be up to the House of Representatives to evaluate the strength of the OIC's evidence. If a majority of the House believed that Clinton may have committed "high crimes and misdemeanors," they would vote to impeach, setting in motion for only the second time in the history of the United States a process the Framers of the Constitution envisioned for dealing with the wrongful conduct of a president.

"THE PEOPLE ARE KING"

Impeachable acts, noted Alexander Hamilton, "are those offenses which proceed from the misconduct of public men, or in other words from the abuse or violation of some public trust."

After further careful consideration, Gouverneur Morris changes his mind on the necessity of impeachments. "The people are King," he declares. Morris suggests that the executive be punished not as a man, but as an officer, and punished only, as Madison recorded, "by degradation from his office."

Eventually, on the question of "Shall the Executive be removable on impeachments?" only the delegates from Massachusetts and South Carolina vote "no." The Connecticut, New Jersey, Pennsylvania, Delaware, Maryland, Virginia, North Carolina, and Georgia delegates all vote "aye."

Once the question of impeaching a sitting president is settled, Madison's preference that the Supreme Court try impeachment cases is overruled. The Framers decide to invest all impeachment power in the legislature.

Yet the Framers recognize the dangers inherent in this arrangement. For the government they envision to

At the Constitutional Convention, James Madison argued that evidence of criminality need not be a prerequisite for impeachment. At the same time, however, he stressed that impeachments should not be based on political considerations.

function properly, neither the legislative nor the executive branch must be dominant. Ideally, the legislature must not be given too much power to remove the president for political reasons.

When "we make the executive amenable to Justice," Gouverneur Morris advises, "we should take care to provide some mode that will not make him dependent on the Legislature." On the other hand, the Framers believe that the legislature shouldn't be able to shield the president from valid impeachment prosecutions either.

Ultimately, the Framers separate the impeachment process into two stages. They make the first stage—charging a president with misconduct that may require his removal from office (strictly speaking, this is what the term "impeachment" means)—the responsibility of the House of Representatives. Article 1, Section 2, Clause 5 of the U.S. Constitution reads, "The House of Representatives shall chuse [choose] their Speaker and other Officers, and shall have the sole Power of Impeachment." A majority vote in the House will be necessary to impeach.

The Framers decide that the second stage of the impeachment process—trial on the charges voted by the House of Representatives—will be the responsibility of the Senate, and a two-thirds majority will be necessary for conviction and removal from office. Article 1, Section 3, Clause 6 of the Constitution reads:

> The Senate shall have the sole Power to try all impeachments. When sitting for that Purpose, they shall be on Oath or Affirmation. When the President of the United States is tried, the Chief Justice shall preside: And no Person shall be convicted without the Concurrence of two thirds of the Members present.

In reporting on the Constitution to the Maryland House of Delegates in November 1787, James McHenry explains that the "power of trying impeachments was lodged in [the Senate] as more likely to be governed by cool and candid investigation, than by those heats that too often inflame and influence the more populous Assemblies."

The Framers must also come to terms with the question of what constitutes an impeachable offense. James Madison thinks "maladministration" too vague a term, allowing a president to serve only at the "pleasure of the Senate." (Just two years later, however, Congressman Madison will claim that it is an abuse of power for a president to remove an officer whose merits require his continuing in office, and that such removal would be an impeachable maladministration of office.) At the Constitutional Convention, Madison argues that evidence of criminality is not required in order to find an impeachable offense, and that

English jurist William Blackstone, the preeminent authority on the common law, greatly influenced America's Founding Fathers.

impeachments should not be based upon political considerations. Colonel Mason eventually withdraws the term "maladministration," and the delegates substitute "high Crimes and Misdemeanors."

On September 12, 1787, the Committee of Style redrafts the impeachment provisions of the Constitution into final form. Article 2, Section 4 of the Constitution reads, "The President, Vice President, and all civil Officers of the United States, shall be removed from Office on Impeachment for, and Conviction of, Treason, Bribery, or other high Crimes and Misdemeanors." The delegates approve the final language just nine days before the new Constitution is signed and transported to the states for the beginning of the ratification process.

Remarkably, however, the Framers never engage in an in-depth debate on the meaning of the phrase "high Crimes and Misdemeanors." At least part of the reason for this may be that they already have an adequate understanding: for the Framers, "high Crimes and Misdemeanors" has a definite, if not precise, meaning derived from hundreds of years of English and colonial usage.

About 30 years before the Constitutional Convention in Philadelphia, Sir William Blackstone published *Commentaries on the Laws of England*, the primary source of authority on the common law (the form of law practiced by the English and largely adopted by the American colonists). At the Virginia convention held to ratify the Framers' newly drafted Constitution, James Madison describes Blackstone's work as "a book which is in every man's hand."

Blackstone differentiated between crimes that "more directly infringe the rights of the public or commonwealth, taken in its collective capacity," and "those which in a more peculiar manner injure individuals or private subjects." Within a subcategory denominated "offenses against the public justice," Blackstone included the crimes of perjury and bribery.

Bribery is generally defined as the tendering or receiving of something of value, an undue reward or advantage, for the purpose of influencing the action of a public official. The Framers list bribery and treason as impeachable acts in the Constitution. Largely because of the English Crown's long history of abuses of power regarding treason prosecutions and convictions, the Framers make treason the only criminal offense defined in the Constitution, requiring that two witnesses testify to the same overt act in open court and limiting what constitutes the offense of treason. Article 3, Section 3 provides:

Article 2, Section 4 of the Constitution provides that the "President, Vice President, and all civil Officers of the United States, shall be removed from Office on Impeachment for, and Conviction of, Treason, Bribery, or other high Crimes and Misdemeanors." The term "high Crimes and Misdemeanors" is not defined.

Treason against the United States, shall consist only in levying War against them, or in adhering to their Enemies, giving them Aid and Comfort. No Person shall be convicted of Treason unless on the Testimony of two Witnesses to the same overt Act, or on Confession in open Court.

The Framers, in their Convention debates leading to the allowance of impeachment for "Treason, Bribery, or other high Crimes and Misdemeanors," only seek to ensure that political passions do not impede or cause impeachment, and that impeachments are not directed at private citizens, as they were for many years before in England.

According to Blackstone, of "high misdemeanors" under English law, the "first and principal one is the maladministration" of office pertaining to the "public trust and employment." Blackstone notes that such maladministration is "usually punished by the method of parliamentary impeachment: wherein such penalties, short of death, are inflicted, as to the wisdom of the house of peers shall seem proper; consisting usually of banishment, imprisonment, fines, or perpetual disability."

Although Blackstone does not discuss the phrase "high crimes and misdemeanors" in any thorough fashion, he devotes a considerable portion of the *Commentaries* to "Public Wrongs," defining public wrongs as "crimes and misdemeanors."

The Framers clearly understand impeachable offenses to be public wrongs. Alexander Hamilton, for example, states that "public wrongs, or crimes and misdemeanors, are a breach and violation of the public rights and duties" that "besides the injury done to individuals, strike at the very being of society," which cannot survive "where actions of this sort" go unpunished. Hamilton further notes that impeachable acts "are those offenses which proceed from the misconduct of public men, or in other words from the abuse or violation of some public trust. They are of a nature which may with peculiar propriety be denominated [political], as they relate chiefly to injuries done immediately to the society itself."

At the Virginia Convention to ratify the Constitution, Governor Randolph speaks of "misbehavior" and "dishonesty" as being impeachable offenses. James Madison gives two examples of impeachable conduct: pardoning a criminal with whom the president was in collusion, and summoning only a few senators to approve a treaty.

At the North Carolina Ratification Convention, James Iredell, who will later serve as a justice of the Supreme Court, speaks of the supremacy of the law under the system of government proposed by the Constitution. "No man has an authority to injure another with impunity," Iredell observes. "No man is better than his fellow-citizens, nor can pretend to any superiority over the meanest man in the country. If the President does a single act, by which the people are prejudiced, he is punishable himself. . . . If he commits any misdemeanor in office, he is impeachable."

Iredell also expresses the view that impeachment may be used only in cases where there is some corrupt motive:

> [W]hen any man is impeached, it must be for an error of the heart, and not of the head. . . . Whatever mistake a man may make, he ought not to be punished for it, nor his posterity rendered infamous. But if a man be a villain, and wilfully abuse his trust, he is to be held up as a public offender, and ignominiously punished. . . . According to these principles, I suppose the only instances in which the President would be liable to impeachment, would be where he had received a bribe, or acted from some corrupt motive or other.

Blackstone explained that "of offences against public justice, some . . . [are] felonious, whose punishment may extend to death; others only misdemeanors." He catalogued those offenses against public justice by beginning "with those that are most penal and descend[ing] gradually to such as are of less malignity." All of these offenses fall short of treason, "the highest civil crime . . . any man can possibly commit," but each constitutes an assault on the "commonwealth or public polity of the kingdom."

Included in Blackstone's catalog of offenses against public justice is "obstructing the execution of lawful process." This "is at all times an offence of a very high and presumptuous nature," and such obstructions of public justice, according to Blackstone, can be of both "the civil and criminal kind."

The history of England's courts and practices of law formed the bases for Blackstone's writings. Armed with Blackstone's book, the Framers did not otherwise need to be experts in the British history of impeachments.

Impeachment originated in the 14th century in England, with indictment by the House of Commons and a trial in the House of Lords. Private citizens and government officeholders alike could be impeached. Impeachable offenses included acts of treason, trespass, and violations of statute, common law, or the king's courts of high commission. A criminal penalty usually followed impeachment, but nearly any offense could serve as an excuse for impeachment.

England's impeachments in precolonial days were often highly politicized, coming most often from power struggles between the king (or queen) and Parliament (England's legislature), and between the political parties the Whigs and the Tories. The American colonies were settled during a time of considerable impeachment activity in England.

Colonists first adopted impeachment out of a sense of responsibility, to protect people from officeholders' abuses of power. When explicitly told by the English authorities to stop the practice of impeachment, the colonists ignored the order and persisted with impeachments during the approximately 140 years before the American Revolution.

In England in the mid-17th century, "high crimes and misdemeanors" began to include such things as negligence and improprieties while in office. Chief Justice William Scroggs, for example, was impeached in 1680 for such acts as browbeating witnesses, cursing and drinking to excess, and generally bringing "the highest scandal on the public justice of the kingdom."

By the 18th century it was clear that English "high crimes and misdemeanors" were not limited to indictable crimes but reached more purely political offenses. In 1701, for example, the earl of Oxford was charged with "violation of his duty and trust." Another British official, Warren Hastings, was charged with maladministration, corruption in office, and cruelty toward the people of India.

From 1701 to 1755, the American colonists began applying impeachment as a "check and balance" against executive and judicial power. In the years just before independence, impeachment also became a tool to resist England's imperial policy and assert American legislative rights against Parliament.

British legal historian William S. Holdsworth commented that the impeachment process was a mechanism in service of the "ideal . . . [of] government in accordance with law." The process was a means by which "the greatest ministers of state could be made responsible, like humble officials, to the law."

Holdsworth believed that "the greatest services rendered by this procedure to the cause of constitutional government have been [the] establishment of the doctrine of ministerial responsibility to the law" and its "application to all ministers" and "consequently the maintenance of the supremacy of the law over all."

America's Founding Fathers understand that the essence of English impeachments was, as Holdsworth would later write, such "misdeeds . . . as peculiarly injure the commonwealth by the abuse of high offices of trust." There was no mistake that the English applied impeachment to persons who were corrupt—abusing official power, misapplying funds, betraying trust, or neglecting duty. And such behavior was often not criminalized.

Impeachments, special noncriminal proceedings under the Constitution, are explicitly made separate from the criminal law by the Framers, who provide for the avoidance of double jeopardy (being tried and exposed to criminal punishment twice for the same offense) by adopting the following language in Article 1, Section 3, Clause 7:

> Judgment in Cases of Impeachment shall not extend further than to removal from Office, and disqualification to hold and enjoy any Office of honor, Trust, or Profit under the United States: but the Party convicted shall nevertheless be liable and subject to Indictment, Trial, Judgment, and Punishment, according to Law.

In avoiding double jeopardy, the Framers express their belief that an act justifying impeachment need not necessarily be a crime. If it is, however, the impeached party's conviction under the constitutional impeachment mechanism is not considered a criminal conviction.

JUDICIAL
IMPEACHMENT

Samuel Chase, associate justice of the U.S. Supreme Court. By potentially undermining the independence of the judiciary, the politically inspired impeachment of Chase threatened the system of checks and balances envisioned by America's Founding Fathers.

When the subject of impeachment comes up, most Americans are likely to think of presidents. In the United States, however, judges have been the most common target of impeachments.

Judge John Pickering of New Hampshire was the first impeached federal official actually convicted. On March 12, 1804, he was found guilty of drunkenness and unlawful rulings.

The precedent set by the Pickering impeachment presented a grave danger to the young country's system of checks and balances among branches of the federal government. If judges could be removed for ruling a certain way on a case, then certain cases could become tainted with political influence from the legislative or executive branch.

A year after Pickering's removal, however, the impeachment of Supreme Court associate justice Samuel Chase established the ability of the judiciary to make independent rulings without fear of legislative interference through threats of removal. A Maryland native and former delegate to the First Continental Congress, Chase had been instrumental in getting the Maryland delegation to vote for complete independence from England in July 1776. Chase was also one of the Maryland signers of the Declaration of Independence. Later, however, he opposed Maryland's ratification of the Constitution because it lacked a Bill of Rights.

Chase's legal skills were widely recognized and respected, but his imperious personality on the bench, along with his strongly held convictions and tendency to dispense severe criticism and biting political opinions, earned him dislike among lawyers, politicians, and fellow judges. Still, Chase was too good a jurist to escape notice. He served as chief judge of the Maryland General Court before George Washington appointed him to the U.S. Supreme Court.

Chase's conduct of several trials once he was on the Supreme Court drew the ire of Republicans—the party of Thomas Jefferson and James Madison. Chase aggravated the situation by remaining in Maryland in August of 1800, after the Supreme Court was supposed to have begun its fall term. He was in Maryland to campaign for the reelection of John Adams—a Federalist opponent of the Republicans—as president.

In May of 1803, Chase criticized the 1802 repeal of the Judiciary Act of 1801, and for good measure he leveled more criticism at various aspects of the Maryland government. This prompted President Thomas Jefferson to write a letter to an influential Maryland congressman, Joseph Nicholson, recommending Chase's impeachment.

Jefferson called Chase's criticism "seditious," strongly implying that Chase had run afoul of the Sedition Act, a law passed in 1798 at a time of strong anti-French feelings. The Sedition Act forbade certain disrespectful criticism of America's government, including

members of Congress, and was passed in large part as a response to discourteous treatment of American ministers in Paris during the late 1790s.

Chase's criticism of the repeal of the Judiciary Act served to remind his political enemies of his other, earlier indiscretions. Eventually seven of the eight articles of impeachment against him pertained to his conduct of trials as a Supreme Court justice while hearing lower "circuit court" federal cases. (In those days and for much of 19th century, a Supreme Court justice would "ride the circuit," traveling by horseback or carriage to different geographic regions to pair up with another federal judge to conduct trials.)

In particular, Chase's conduct at trials in Philadelphia, Richmond, and Delaware in 1800, and his charge

The acquittal of Samuel Chase on impeachment charges, wrote Chief Justice William Rehnquist (above), established the crucial precedent that "impeachment would not be used to remove members of the Supreme Court for their judicial opinions."

to a grand jury in Baltimore in 1803—prompting Jefferson's letter—became the focus of his impeachment trial. The trial began in February of 1805.

The charge to the grand jury seemed to present a question that could not be answered merely by analyzing law or proper trial technique, colonial or English common law history, or case precedents. What Chase actually said was not precisely recorded, but the critical language of the charge involved the following:

> You know, gentlemen, that our state and national institutions were framed to secure to every member of the society equal liberty and equal rights; but the late alteration of the federal judiciary, by the abolition of the office of the sixteen circuit judges, and the recent change in our state constitution by the establishing of universal suffrage, and the further alteration that is contemplated in our state judiciary . . . will in my judgment take away all security for property and personal liberty. . . . The independence of the judges of this state will be entirely destroyed, if the bill for abolishing the two supreme courts should be ratified by the next general assembly. The change of the state constitution by allowing universal suffrage will in my opinion certainly and rapidly destroy all protection to property, and all security to personal liberty; and our Republican constitution will sink into a mobocracy, the worst of all possible governments.

At his impeachment trial Chase responded by answering that he repented of giving the "unfounded" and "incorrect" opinions, but that there was no law that forbade his giving them. In addition, he said, it was common for a judge to express from the bench, by way of a charge (instruction) to the grand jury, such political opinions as the judge thought useful and correct.

At the time, the federal government of America was only 15 years old. Whether a judge should let his political views play a part in his charges to a grand jury was not a complex legal question but had no easy answer.

The fact that Chase criticized the Maryland government was, to the Jeffersonian Republicans—who were advocates of strong state power, as opposed to a strong federal government—even worse than Chase's criticism directed at the federal government. Ultimately, however, Chase's trial conduct and grand jury handling and his criticism of federal and Maryland government actions were found to be less than impeachable offenses. On Chase's criticism of government, the Senate voted 19 to 15 in favor of conviction, the largest margin of any vote on the eight articles, but four votes short of the necessary two-thirds majority.

Chief Justice William H. Rehnquist wrote in his 1992 book *Grand Inquests* that the acquittal of Chase served two important purposes. First, it ensured "the independence of federal judges from congressional oversight of the decisions they made in the cases that came before them." Second, it established that "impeachment would not be used to remove members of the Supreme Court for their judicial opinions," helping to "safeguard the independence of that body."

A test of judicial independence quickly followed Chase's acquittal when former vice president Aaron Burr became the subject of a criminal indictment. The day after Chase was acquitted, Burr delivered a farewell speech to the Senate, then disappeared from public life. He reportedly traveled as far west as Ohio and the Mississippi River. In those days, there were constant political movements among "frontiersmen" to change or improve the government, including efforts to secede (separate) from the United States. Such efforts cropped up among persons living in the territory south of the Ohio River, between the Mississippi River to the west and the Appalachian Mountains to the east.

During his wanderings, Burr visited a wealthy pioneer named Harman Blennerhassett near present-day Parkersburg, West Virginia. Blennerhassett later advocated, in several writings, Burr's idea of separating the states west of the Appalachians (including Tennessee, Kentucky, and Ohio) from the United States.

In 1807, President Thomas Jefferson publicly identified Burr, a political enemy of his, as the leader of a
secession conspiracy—and possibly of a conspiracy to
wage war on Spain—and proclaimed Burr guilty
"beyond question." Burr was captured by federal mar-
shals and taken on horseback to Richmond. There
Chief Justice John Marshall presided over Burr's
arraignment (a formal bringing of charges).

Marshall ruled against the government's preliminary motion, deciding that Burr could not be held to
answer for the capital crime of treason but could be
tried for treason as a high misdemeanor. Justice Marshall released Burr on bail after setting a trial date, all
to President Jefferson's great displeasure.

The proceedings against Burr were held in the Virginia House of Delegates. After a grand jury indicted
Burr for treason, President Jefferson took an active role
in urging Burr's prosecutor, George Hay, the U.S. Attorney for Virginia, to obtain a conviction. Jefferson's
attempt to inject political influence into the process
was clearly at odds with two of the Framers' goals: the
separation of power among branches of government,
and the avoidance of politicized impeachments.

Despite Jefferson's harsh stance and vigorous efforts,
the trial was conducted fairly. Marshall eventually
ruled, in effect, that the United States had not proven
treason as defined in the Constitution. The jury
returned a vote of "not guilty" on the charge of treason.

Burr's acquittal may have been in large part a by-
product of Chase's acquittal. As Rehnquist pointed out
in *Grand Inquests*, it was far easier for Marshall to act
with complete independence, refusing to yield to the
president's pressure and influence, with the precedent
of Chase's acquittal firmly establishing an independent
judiciary.

Although judges have been largely shielded from
political pressure over their legal decisions, they have
not been immune to impeachment and removal for

actions outside the courtroom. In some cases the impeachable conduct has been criminal, but in other instances it has merely been deemed to violate ethical standards. One instance of noncriminal conduct that led to impeachment and removal was the case of Tennessee federal judge West H. Humphreys. In 1862 Humphreys accepted an appointment as a judge of the Confederate States of America—the Southern states at war with the Union—without resigning his federal judgeship. He was quickly impeached by a voice vote in the House and, when he failed to appear before the Senate to answer the charges, unanimously removed in June 1862.

More recently, federal judge Alcee Hastings was impeached and removed for soliciting a bribe, despite the fact that a federal criminal jury had already acquitted him of the same charge. The Senate voted 69 to 26 to convict Hastings, a judge for the U.S. District Court for the Southern District of Florida, removing him in 1989.

U.S. District Court judge Walter Nixon was also impeached and removed from office in 1989. Nixon, however, *had* been convicted of a crime, but he had then failed to resign his judgeship. The charges against Nixon would find an echo a decade later, in the case against President Clinton: Nixon was convicted and removed for perjury—specifically, lying to a federal grand jury. Independent Counsel Kenneth Starr alleged that Clinton had committed this same offense. Interestingly, the president's legal team would argue that even if true, the article of impeachment concerning perjury before the grand jury did not present an impeachable offense meeting the standard of "high crimes and misdemeanors."

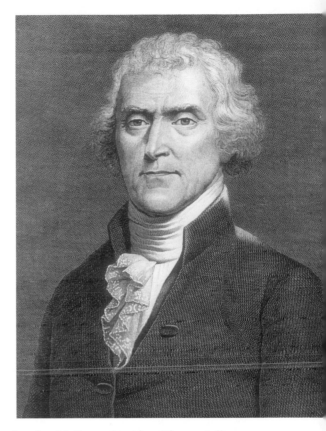

President Thomas Jefferson (above) attempted to use his influence to ensure the conviction of his political enemy Aaron Burr on treason charges. But Chief Justice John Marshall—reassured, perhaps, by the results of the Chase impeachment—conducted the trial fairly, and Burr was acquitted.

THE FIRST PRESIDENTIAL IMPEACHMENT

In 1998 and 1999, many supporters of President Clinton characterized the case against him as a politically motivated incursion into the president's private life. One hundred thirty years earlier, the first presidential impeachment had most certainly been politically motivated. But unlike the sex-and-lies scandal that formed the basis for the charges against Clinton, the case against Andrew Johnson had centered on speeches and administrative decisions Johnson had made in his role as president. In that respect it bore a greater resemblance to the impeachment of Justice Samuel Chase than to the impeachment of President William Jefferson Clinton.

Johnson didn't stand accused of criminal offenses. Rather, the controversy essentially involved the discretion and authority of the president to interpret a point of law independently, without too much congressional oversight backed by the threat of impeachment and removal.

A photo of the seven House managers who served as prosecutors during the impeachment trial of President Andrew Johnson in 1868.

Johnson's dismissal of Secretary of War Edwin Stanton (above)—in supposed violation of the Tenure of Office Act—inspired his political enemies to press for his impeachment and removal.

In 1861, Senator Andrew Johnson of Tennessee had condemned the South's secession and refused to follow his state into the Confederacy. Johnson's status as the only Southern member of Congress who remained loyal to the Union won him great acclaim in the North.

But Johnson supported the Union's war on the South only insofar as its goal was to reunite the country. He was coauthor of the Crittendon-Johnson Resolution, passed by Congress in the summer of 1861. The resolution explained that the sole aim of the Civil War was the restoration of the Union, not interference with any Southern state's domestic institutions—which of course referred to the institution of slavery.

Johnson, born in Raleigh, North Carolina, in 1808, had risen from abject poverty to become the owner, at age 19, of his own tailor shop in the eastern Tennessee town of Greeneville. Eastern Tennessee had few slaveholders, unlike the middle and western parts of the state, and strongly but unsuccessfully supported the Union immediately before secession.

Abraham Lincoln selected Johnson as his running mate in 1864, and Johnson was sworn in as vice president at Lincoln's second inauguration in March of 1865. At the inauguration, Johnson's speech failed to make a good impression on many listeners. Taking whiskey shortly before his appearance to soothe an illness, Johnson appeared drunk.

After Lincoln's assassination in April 1865, Johnson became president. Despite his status as a hero for his stance on secession, Johnson quickly managed to make a large group of political enemies in Congress.

Some of the most fervent of those enemies were the "Radical Republicans," who favored conditioning approval of any Reconstruction plan—that is, any plan to readmit the Southern states into the Union—upon their giving the vote to the freed slaves.

By 1867 Congress and President Johnson were bitterly squabbling. In January, Johnson's conduct was made the subject of a congressional investigation. In February, the House Judiciary Committee began hearing testimony on the appropriateness of impeachment.

In March, Congress passed the Tenure of Office Act, prohibiting presidential removal of any federal official whose appointment required Senate confirmation. It was unclear whether the new law applied to a cabinet member appointed by a previous president, because the law read in pertinent part that cabinet members "shall hold their offices . . . during the term of the President by whom they may have been appointed . . . subject to removal by and with the advice and consent of the Senate."

Edwin Stanton had become attorney general in President James Buchanan's cabinet on December 27, 1860—the day when Congress received news of the relocation of the garrison at Fort Moultrie in Charleston Harbor to the more defensible Fort Sumter, a prelude to the Civil War. Stanton served as secretary of war in Johnson's cabinet until Johnson suspended him from his post in August of 1867, while Congress was in recess. When the Senate reconvened in January, a month after the House motion to impeach Johnson on other matters had failed by a vote of 108 to 57, the Senate voted 35 to 16 against concurrence with Stanton's removal. Stanton was reinstated as secretary of war.

On February 21, 1868, Johnson again directed the removal of Stanton and informed the Senate of his decision. A Senate resolution was immediately passed, denying the president's power to remove Stanton. In the House late that afternoon, it appeared certain that

This page: President Andrew Johnson. Opposite page: Facsimile of an admission ticket to Johnson's impeachment trial in the Senate.

an impeachment resolution would pass once the members received an opportunity to speak. The resolution that passed 126-47 three days later, along party lines, lacked any specificity: "Resolved, That Andrew Johnson, President of the United States, be impeached of high crimes and misdemeanors."

The Senate took no action on the nomination of Stanton's replacement. Meanwhile, Stanton, with the help of armed volunteers, maintained a 24-hour vigil at the War Department. The House initially drafted 10 articles of impeachment, all but 2 of which pertained to Johnson's attempt to remove Stanton contrary to the Tenure of Office Act. An 11th article was later added.

Articles I, IV, V, VI, VII, and VIII accused Johnson

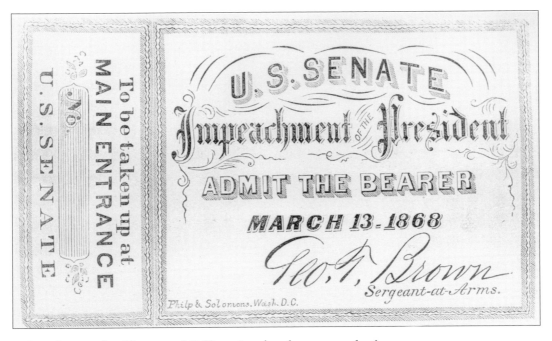

of violating the Tenure of Office Act by the removal of
Stanton. Articles II and III accused the president of
unlawfully designating an interim secretary of war to
replace Stanton. Article IX's charge concerned Johnson's alleged attempt to induce General William Emory
to disobey an act of Congress requiring Senate approval
for the removal of the General of the Army. Article X
concerned various disparaging statements Johnson had
made about congressmen and the Congress during public speeches. And Article XI was a general compilation
of the charges that attempted to, as Chief Justice
William Rehnquist wrote in his book *Grand Inquests*,
"cast a broader net."

The trial began on March 30, 1868. On Saturday,
April 4, the House managers—congressmen who had
been assigned the task of acting as prosecutors during
the Senate trial—finished presenting the documentary
evidence and calling witnesses. After a five-day post-
ponement, the president's attorneys presented the
defense, concluding on April 20. Closing arguments
began April 22. The impeachment trial would continue

for more than six weeks.

The case fundamentally concerned the Tenure of Office Act. To convict on Articles II and III, the Senate needed to conclude that statutes passed in 1792 and 1795 were repealed by implication in a statute passed in 1862. Testimony pertinent to Article IX showed that Johnson did no more than express grave doubts to Emory regarding the constitutionality of the law in question.

Article X was impossible to successfully prosecute, as no transcripts of Johnson's speeches existed, and anyway the First Amendment to the Constitution—prohibiting Congress from making any law "abridging the freedom of speech"—stood as an incontrovertible barrier to the charge that Johnson could have committed an impeachable offense during speech making.

Ultimately it was very difficult to argue that any of the articles of impeachment against Johnson described a "high crime or misdemeanor." The president's defense consisted of three main arguments: (1) Stanton was not covered by the Tenure of Office Act; (2) if he was covered by it, the point was in significant controversy and so obscure that it should not be the basis for removal of the president; and (3) the act itself unconstitutionally violated the power granted to the chief executive by the Constitution in Article 2 to "take care that the laws be faithfully executed."

One of the sections of the act provided that violation of its terms was a "high misdemeanor." The Senate passage of the act excluded coverage of cabinet members. The House amended the bill to include the cabinet. Ultimately a compromise was adopted that seemed to indicate that members of Andrew Johnson's cabinet originally appointed by Lincoln—as Stanton was—were not covered.

The Republican senators who voted to acquit were most swayed by the argument, advanced by the president's counsel, that the Tenure of Office Act's coverage was so vague and unclear as to be essentially uninterpretable. Under those circumstances, how could the president be convicted of intentionally violating the law? (The Tenure of Office Act was ultimately repealed nearly 20 years later.)

On May 16 the Senate passed a resolution to vote on Article XI first, and the vote fell one short of the number needed for conviction. The Senate then passed a resolution to adjourn for 10 days. When the senators returned and voted on Articles II and III, each article fell one vote short of the two-thirds majority needed to convict. By a vote of 34 to 16, the Senate then voted to adjourn for good as a court of impeachment, never voting on the remaining articles.

In written opinions, 30 of the 34 Republican senators who participated in the trial explained their views. Senator William Pitt Fessenden of Maine thought that removing a president for putting the wrong interpretation on a statute would be an abuse of the Senate's power. In a letter written after the end of the trial, Senator James Dixon of Connecticut observed that impeachment had not become "an ordinary means of changing the policy of the government by a violent removal of the executive."

However, the first impeachment trial of a president had been highly politicized. In fact, Johnson was impeached out of dislike by political foes after an earlier attempt to formulate articles of impeachment had failed. And he escaped conviction and removal under three separate articles by just one vote.

CLINTON
IMPEACHED

After the Office of Independent Counsel had submitted its referral to Congress listing 11 possible grounds for the impeachment of President Clinton, responsibility for deciding how to proceed rested with the House of Representatives. On September 18, 1998, the House passed—with overwhelming bipartisan support—a resolution directing the Judiciary Committee to review the Starr Report.

In a statement on the House floor, Judiciary Committee chairman Henry Hyde summed up his understanding of the task before him and his colleagues: "We are here to ask this one simple question: based upon what we now know, do we have a duty to look further, or to look away." The members of Hyde's committee—21 Republicans and 16 Democrats—decided that they had a duty to look further, voting unanimously to conduct some kind of investigation.

That early show of unanimity did not signal a last-

Flanked by boxes of evidence from Kenneth Starr's OIC investigation, House Judiciary Committee chairman Henry Hyde holds a press conference. At left is Rep. Mary Bono, another Republican member of the Judiciary Committee.

ing spirit of bipartisanship, however. Republicans and Democrats on the Judiciary Committee squabbled bitterly over rules, procedures, and even the basic goal of their work. Claiming that the investigation of President Clinton had gone on too long already, Democrats argued against prolonged committee hearings. The Democrats even suggested that before the Judiciary Committee proceeded to examine evidence, it should first determine what constituted impeachable conduct and whether the alleged wrongdoing in the Starr Report met the criteria. Republicans rejected this suggestion.

The midterm congressional elections on November 3—in which the Democrats fared surprisingly well, gaining five House seats—changed the equation. Exit polls suggested that voters had become increasingly disenchanted with the investigation of Clinton and largely blamed the Republicans. Two-thirds said they didn't want Clinton impeached. The Judiciary Committee Democrats now called for a thorough examination, while the Republicans backed down and urged a more "expeditious" process. Ultimately Chairman Hyde committed to having the impeachment hearings completed by the end of 1998.

These time constraints prevented the committee from calling any material witnesses, such as Lewinsky, Tripp, Currie, or Jordan. In the interests of expediting the process and establishing a factual basis upon which to proceed, the committee submitted 81 written questions to President Clinton, including: "Do you admit or deny that you gave false and misleading testimony under oath when you stated during your deposition in the case of *Jones v. Clinton* on January 17, 1998, that you did not know if Monica Lewinsky had been subpoenaed to testify in that case?" and "Do you admit or deny that on or about December 28, 1997, you requested, instructed, suggested to or otherwise discussed with Betty Currie that she take possession of gifts previously given to Monica Lewinsky by you?" Clinton's failure to answer these questions to the satisfaction of committee Republicans—who complained that rather than trying to clarify the record he had chosen to "stick with his reliance on bizarre technical definitions and legalistic defenses"—would ultimately form the basis of an impeachment charge for obstruction of justice. As Judiciary Committee chairman Henry Hyde would remark, "The President may have been under no legal obligation to be helpful to Paula Jones, but he is under a strong legal obligation to be helpful and cooperative with the congressional Committee charged with investigating impeachment."

Of the witnesses who did testify before the Judiciary Committee, Independent Counsel Starr was the most controversial. Under hostile questioning from committee Democrats and friendly questioning from committee Republicans, Starr defended his inquiry. Clinton lawyer Charles Ruff presented a defense for the president, although he complained that the committee had not

Kenneth Starr testifies before the House Judiciary Committee, November 19, 1998.

even given him a list of the charges before his testimony. Other witnesses included a panel of former federal prosecutors (called by committee Democrats) who testified that perjury is rarely prosecuted in civil cases, and a pair of women (called by committee Republicans) who were prosecuted for and convicted of perjury.

Although Democrats complained that the failure to call material witnesses and thoroughly examine the evidence presented in the Starr Report constituted a rush to judgment, Republicans insisted that their role in the impeachment process was analogous to that of a grand jury in a criminal case: they merely decided whether enough evidence existed to "indict," not whether there was enough evidence to obtain a conviction. On December 11 and 12, the Judiciary Committee voted, along party lines, to approve four articles

of impeachment to be sent to the full House of Representatives for consideration.

Article I charged Clinton with perjury during his
August 17, 1998, testimony before the federal grand
jury. Article II alleged perjury in Clinton's written
answers (denying sexual relations with any subordinate
employee after 1986) during discovery and again during
his deposition in the Jones lawsuit. Article III listed
seven acts or schemes in which Clinton allegedly
engaged to obstruct justice, including encouraging
Monica Lewinsky to file a false affidavit in the Jones
case, attempting to conceal evidence (the gifts he had
given Lewinsky) in the Jones case, attempting to secure
a job for Lewinsky to influence her testimony, and giving false and misleading information to aides and cabinet members with the knowledge that they might be
called to testify before the grand jury, where they would
then pass on the false information. The final article
charged that Clinton had abused the power of his office
by refusing to answer some of the 81 written questions
posed to him by the Judiciary Committee and by
answering others falsely.

On December 19, 1998, the full House of Representatives rejected the second and fourth articles but
voted to send Articles I and III to the Senate. The
impeachment trial would begin in January, with the
core charges against the president involving perjury
and obstruction of justice.

Perjury, the basis for the first impeachment article
against President Clinton, has four general elements: (1)
an oath, (2) intent, (3) falsity, and (4) materiality. The
oath need not be administered in any particular form,
but it must be administered by a legally authorized person. The intent element requires that false testimony be
knowingly stated or subscribed, and this element is sat-
isfied by proof that the defendant knew his testimony
was false at the time it was provided. In the absence of
an admission by the defendant, the prosecution must

rely upon circumstantial evidence to prove intent. The element of falsity requires that a defendant must actually make one or more false statements to be convicted of perjury. The final element of perjury, materiality, requires the prosecution to prove that the statement passes the Supreme Court's test of whether it had "a natural tendency to influence" or was "capable of influencing" the official proceeding. A false statement about something unrelated or only peripherally related to an issue in question does not constitute perjury. However, the law also makes clear that the false statement does

Articles of Impeachment Against President Clinton

Article I (approved 228-206) alleged that "on August 17, 1998, William Jefferson Clinton swore to tell the truth . . . before a Federal grand jury of the United States," and contrary to that oath "willfully provided perjurious, false and misleading testimony to the grand jury concerning one or more of the following: (1) the nature and details of his relationship with a subordinate Government employee; (2) prior perjurious, false and misleading testimony he gave in a Federal civil rights action brought against him; (3) prior false and misleading statements he allowed his attorney to make to a Federal judge in that civil rights action; and (4) his corrupt efforts to influence the testimony of witnesses and to impede the discovery of evidence."

Article II (rejected 229-205) alleged: "(1) On December 23, 1997, William Jefferson Clinton, in sworn answers to written questions asked as part of a Federal civil rights action brought against him, willfully provided perjurious, false and misleading testimony in response to questions deemed relevant by a Federal judge concerning conduct and proposed conduct with subordinate employees. (2) On January 17, 1998, [Clinton] swore under oath to tell the truth . . . in a deposition given as part of a Federal civil rights action brought against him. Contrary to that oath [he] willfully provided perjurious, false and misleading testimony in response to questions deemed relevant by a Federal judge concerning the nature and details of his relationship with a subordinate Government employee and his corrupt efforts to influence the testimony of that employee."

Article III (approved 221-212) listed seven acts or schemes demonstrating that Clinton "prevented, obstructed, and impeded the administration of justice, and has to that end engaged personally, and through his subordinates and agents" he delayed, covered up, and concealed "the existence of evidence and testimony related to a Federal civil rights action brought against him in a duly instituted judicial proceeding." These acts included allegations that Clinton: (1) "[o]n or about December 17, 1997 . . . corruptly encouraged a witness . . . to execute a sworn affidavit in that proceeding that he knew to be perjurious, false and misleading"; (2) "corruptly encouraged a witness . . . to give perjurious, false and not have to actually impede a grand jury's investigation for the statement to be material. The closely related offense of subornation of perjury, which Article III alleged Clinton had committed, was succinctly defined in the 18th century by Sir William Blackstone as "the offence of procuring another to take such a false oath, as constitutes perjury in the principal."

Blackstone found perjury and subornation of perjury to be "detestable" crimes. Such offenses were previously punishable by death, but by his era conviction merely earned "six months imprisonment, perpetual infamy,

misleading testimony if and when called to testify personally in that proceeding"; (3) "[o]n or about December 28, 1997. . . corruptly engaged in, encouraged, or supported a scheme to conceal evidence that had been subpoenaed in a Federal civil rights action brought against him"; (4) "[b]eginning on or about December 7, 1997, and continuing through and including January 14, 1998, intensified and succeeded in an effort to secure job assistance to a witness . . . in order to corruptly prevent the truthful testimony of that witness . . . when the truthful testimony of that witness would have been harmful to him"; (5) "[o]n January 17, 1998, at his deposition . . . corruptly allowed his attorney to make false and misleading statements to a Federal judge . . . in order to prevent questioning deemed relevant by the judge"; (6) "[o]n or about January 18 and January 20–21, 1998 . . . related a false and misleading account of events . . . to a potential witness . . . in order to corruptly influence the testimony of that witness"; and (7) "[o]n or about January 21, 23 and 26, 1998 . . . made false and misleading statements to potential witnesses . . . in order to corruptly influence the testimony of those witnesses," and those false and misleading statements were later "repeated by the witnesses to the grand jury, causing the grand jury to receive false and misleading information."

According to Article IV (rejected 285-140), Clinton allegedly misused and abused "his high office, impaired the due and proper administration of justice and the conduct of lawful inquiries, and contravened the authority of the legislative branch and the truth-seeking purpose of a coordinate investigative proceeding" by having "refused and failed to respond to certain written requests for admission and willfully made perjurious, false and misleading sworn statements in response to certain written requests for admission propounded to him as part of the impeachment inquiry authorized by the House of Representatives of the Congress of the United States. . . . [I]n refusing and failing to respond, and in making perjurious, false and misleading statements, [he] assumed to himself functions and judgments necessary to the exercise of the sole power of impeachment vested by the Constitution in the House of Representatives and exhibited contempt for the inquiry."

The House Judiciary Committee in the midst of voting on proposed articles of impeachment against President Clinton. The committee sent four articles to the full House. Two were approved.

and a . . . fine, or to have both ears nailed to the pillory." In Blackstone's hierarchy, perjury is followed immediately by the crime of bribery.

Nearly 200 years after Blackstone, the United States Supreme Court observed that "perjured testimony is an obvious and flagrant affront to the basic concepts of judicial proceedings. Effective restraints against this type of egregious offense are therefore imperative."

According to the Supreme Court, a false statement made in a civil administrative proceeding "is intolerable. We must neither reward nor condone such a 'flagrant affront' to the truth-seeking function of adversary proceedings. . . . Perjury should be severely sanctioned in appropriate cases."

While perjury, subornation of perjury, and the other charge for which Clinton was impeached—obstruction of justice—are distinct offenses, they are variations on a single theme: preventing the discovery of truth. *Black's Law Dictionary* defines obstruction of justice as "[i]mpeding or obstructing those who seek justice in a court, or those who have duties or powers of administering justice therein." Obstruction of justice, like perjury, is a crime in the federal criminal code. Federal sentencing guidelines increase the sentence of a convicted defendant who has "willfully obstructed or impeded, or attempted to obstruct or impede, the administration of justice during the investigation, prosecution, or sentencing" of his or her offense. According to the sentencing guidelines, examples of obstruction include "committing, suborning, or attempting to suborn perjury" and "destroying or concealing or directing or procuring another person to destroy or conceal evidence that is material to an official investigation or judicial proceeding."

The Articles of Impeachment stated that the president:

> In his conduct while President of the United States . . . in violation of his constitutional oath faithfully to execute the office of President of the United States and, to the best of his ability, preserve, protect, and defend the Constitution of the United States, and in violation of his constitutional duty to take care that the laws be faithfully executed, has willfully corrupted and manipulated the judicial process of the United States for his personal gain and exoneration, impeding the administration of justice.

Clinton on Trial

On January 6, 1999, the House voted to appoint 13 House managers, all Republican members of the Judiciary Committee, to prosecute the case against the president. The next morning, Henry Hyde led the managers to the Senate chamber to open the impeachment trial of President Clinton, during which 55 Republicans and 45 Democrats would be charged with the solemn responsibility of deciding whether, for the first time in American history, a president should be removed from office for wrongdoing.

When South Carolina's 96-year-old senator, Strom Thurmond, called the Senate to order, there was as yet no agreement on how to conduct the trial. Procedural rules adopted by the Senate during President Johnson's impeachment in 1868 were followed for the opening. After Hyde read the articles of impeachment to the Senate, the proceedings were adjourned until the afternoon. At that time, Chief Justice Rehnquist, and then the entire Senate, was sworn in. The proceedings were

A binder containing the two articles of impeachment against President Clinton sits on the desk of Gary Sisco, secretary of the Senate, after being delivered by Republican members of the House Judiciary Committee, December 19, 1998.

then adjourned once again.

Later in the afternoon, following several hours of discussion, Senate majority leader Trent Lott and Democratic leader Tom Daschle appeared together and announced that the Senate would meet the next morning to vote on a bipartisan agreement on the impeachment trial procedure. The Senate convened late in the afternoon, and a Senate clerk read aloud the details of the agreement to the sitting senators. The agreement called for the trial to resume on Wednesday, January 13, to consider any motions filed by either party. The House managers would then have up to 24 hours to present their case. Next, the president's legal team would get the same amount of time to present the defense. Finally, the Senate would have up to 16 hours to submit written questions to both sides. A motion to dispose of the trial would then be in order, and if the motion failed to garner a simple majority, motions to present witnesses or evidence not in the record would be recognized. Following closing arguments, the Senate would then vote on the two articles of impeachment. The vote to proceed accordingly passed the Senate 100-0.

Two days before the trial resumed, the White House attorneys issued a 13-page response to the impeachment summons. Basically, this document presented a two-pronged defense strategy that the president's legal team would follow throughout the remainder of the impeachment process. The first prong was a refutation of the specific charges of perjury and obstruction of justice contained in the impeachment articles. The second prong attempted to demonstrate that the offenses alleged weren't serious enough to be impeachable anyway, and that to remove the president under the circumstances would do terrible damage to the presidency and the country.

In denying the charge of perjury before the grand jury stemming from the president's insistence that he had answered the questions of Paula Jones's lawyers

truthfully during his deposition, the defense document stated that Clinton "specifically acknowledged to the grand jury that he had an improper intimate relationship with Ms. Lewinsky." However, as he explained during his grand jury testimony, he had not engaged in sexual relations with her as he understood that term to be defined during the Jones deposition. Furthermore, the president had admitted to the grand jury that he had been trying not to assist Jones's lawyers.

In the matter of "statements he allowed his attorney to make" during the Jones deposition, the president once again denied he had committed perjury. He claimed that he "was truthful when he explained to the grand jury his understanding of certain statements made by his lawyer, Robert Bennett, during the Jones deposition" and also truthful "when he testified that he

Chief Justice William Rehnquist presides over the Senate trial of William Jefferson Clinton.

Henry Hyde, leader of the House managers, makes the case before the Senate for convicting President Clinton.

was not focusing on the prolonged and complicated exchange between the attorneys and Judge Wright."

The president also denied that he made efforts "to influence the testimony of witnesses and to impede the discovery of evidence" as alleged in Article I.

In denying the charges in Article II (the Judiciary Committee's Article III), the president made various factual responses, including statements denying that he "corruptly encouraged" Lewinsky "to execute a sworn affidavit in that proceeding that he knew to be perjurious, false and misleading." The president cited the testimony and proffered statements of Lewinsky, "the only witness cited in support of this allegation" as proof. Lewinsky testified, "No one ever asked me to lie and I was never promised a job for my silence."

The president's defense acknowledged that "prior to

Ms. Lewinsky's involvement in the Jones case, he and Ms. Lewinsky might have talked about what to do to conceal their relationship from others" but that "Ms. Lewinsky was not a witness in any legal proceeding at that time."

> Ms. Lewinsky's own testimony and statements support the President's recollection. Ms. Lewinsky testified that she "pretty much can" exclude the possibility that she and the President ever had discussions about denying the relationship after she learned she was a witness in the Jones case. Ms. Lewinsky also stated that "they did not discuss the issue [of what to say about their relationship] in specific relation to the Jones matter," and that "she does not believe they discussed the content of any deposition that [she] might be involved in at a later date."

The president also denied that he "corruptly engaged in, encouraged, or supported a scheme to conceal evidence" in the Jones case. This charge referred to the gifts Clinton had given Lewinsky, which were supposed to have been turned over to the court but which ended up under Betty Currie's bed. Clinton maintained that he had not asked Currie to retrieve the gifts. "Ms. Currie," his lawyers' statement said, "told prosecutors as early as January 1998 and repeatedly thereafter that it was Ms. Lewinsky who had contacted her about retrieving gifts." Nor had the president, according to his lawyers, ever encouraged or suggested that Lewinsky conceal the gifts. In fact, the trial brief said, when Lewinsky asked what to do if she were asked in the Jones case about the gifts, "the President responded that she would have to turn over whatever she had."

Responding to the charge that efforts to obtain Lewinsky a job in New York were made to "corruptly prevent" her "truthful testimony" in the Jones case and thus amounted to obstruction of justice, the president stated that the job search had no "connection whatsoever to Ms. Lewinsky's status as a possible or actual witness in the Jones case." Not only had "he discussed with

Ms. Lewinsky her desire to obtain a job in New York months before she was listed as a potential witness in the Jones case," but "Ms. Lewinsky was offered a job in New York at the United Nations more than a month before she was identified as a possible witness." The president also stated that he believed it had been Lewinsky's idea to enlist Vernon Jordan's help in her job search, a recollection she corroborated. In addition, the president's lawyers argued, her testimony that "I was never promised a job for my silence" confirmed the president's innocence.

Another alleged obstruction of justice centered on the conversation Clinton had with Betty Currie on January 18, 1998, after his deposition in the Jones case. The president denied he had been trying to influence Currie's potential testimony when he asked her questions such as "Monica came on to me and I never touched her, right?" Rather, he insisted that he had been "trying to find out what the facts were, what Ms. Currie's perception was, and whether his own recollection was correct about certain aspects of his relationship with Ms. Lewinsky." In support of that argument, Clinton's trial brief said that "Ms. Currie testified that she felt no pressure 'whatsoever' from the President's statements and no pressure 'to agree with [her] boss,'" and that the president at the time did not know or believe that Ms. Currie would be a witness in any relevant proceeding. "[A]fter the Independent Counsel investigation became public, when Ms. Currie was scheduled to testify," the defense brief stated, "he told Ms. Currie to 'tell the truth.'"

Finally, the president denied that he had intended to influence the grand jury investigation when he misled his aides—and the nation—about the nature of his relationship with Monica Lewinsky after the press broke the story on January 21, 1998. Rather, he had wanted only "to avoid disclosing his personal wrongdoing to protect his family and himself from hurt and public embarrassment."

In the second prong of their defense, the president's lawyers asserted that the phrase "Treason, Bribery or other high Crimes and Misdemeanors strongly suggests . . . that, to be impeachable offenses, high crimes and misdemeanors must be of the seriousness of 'Treason' and 'Bribery.'" To remove a president for something less, they argued, "would defy the constitutional presumption that the removal power rests with the people in elections, and it would do incalculable damage to the institution of the Presidency."

The standard for impeaching and removing judges, the president's lawyers argued, was different because judges can't be removed from office at the polls. So while it might be legitimate to impeach and remove a judge for lesser offenses, removing the president requires wrongdoing of much greater seriousness. The president's attorneys reasoned that since the Framers "made the President the sole nationally elected public official (together with the Vice-President), responsible to all the people," upon impeachment

> the Senate confronts this inescapable question: is the alleged misconduct so profoundly serious, so malevolent to our Constitutional system, that it justifies undoing the people's decision? Is the wrong alleged of a sort that not only demands removal of the President before the ordinary electoral cycle can do its work, but also justifies the national trauma that accompanies the impeachment trial process itself? The wrongdoing alleged here does not remotely meet that standard.

Besides maintaining that Clinton's alleged wrongdoing was insufficiently serious to warrant overturning an election, his lawyers offered another argument against removal: his conduct had been private. According to the defense, the Framers had intended impeachments only as "a method of removing a President whose continued presence in the Office would cause grave danger to the Nation and our Constitutional system of government," and that "in all but the most extreme

When the Senate voted to limit witness testimony to three videotaped depositions, the House managers chose Monica Lewinsky, Vernon Jordan, and White House adviser Sidney Blumenthal. No major revelations emerged from the depositions.

instances, impeachment should be limited to abuse of public office, not private misconduct unrelated to public office." As the president's lawyers pointed out, even the House managers acknowledged that "the President's [alleged] perjury and obstruction do not directly involve his official conduct."

On January 14, 1999, the House managers filed a rebuttal to Clinton's defense. They asserted that the president's defense memorandum contained "numerous factual inaccuracies and misstatements of the governing law and the Senate's precedents."

"To the extent that President Clinton's Trial Memorandum raises issues of credibility," the House managers declared, "those issues are best resolved by live testimony subject to cross-examination. The Senate, weighing the evidence in its entirety, will make an independent assessment of the facts as they are presented, and a detailed, point-by-point argument on these matters is best resolved on the Senate floor. The House is confident that a thorough factual analysis will not only refute President Clinton's contentions, but will prove the very serious charges contained in the articles."

Whether or not witnesses should testify live during the Senate trial would become a key point of contention. Earlier, the president's lawyers had offered to forego their rights to test the credibility of Starr's witnesses through cross-examination if the House managers agreed not to call any witnesses at the Senate trial. This offer, the president's lawyers claimed, was "based on what we think is our ability to argue this case [exclusively on the evidence contained in the Starr Report], and based on the overwhelming consensus that it is in the best interests of this country and the American people to find a way to put this whole case behind us." And, as White House spokesperson Joe Lockhart pointed out, the House hadn't felt it needed live witnesses during its impeachment debate. The House managers, however, reiterated their argument that the House had fulfilled its proper role in impeachment—to decide whether sufficient grounds existed to hold a Senate trial—and they maintained that "Senate precedents firmly establish that the Senate has always fulfilled its responsibility to give a full and fair hearing to articles of impeachment voted by the House of Representatives."

As for the president's claim that his alleged misconduct didn't rise to the level of a high crime or misdemeanor, the House managers stated that the Constitution sets one standard for impeachment, and the "Senate has repeatedly determined that perjury [meets that standard]" and that "obstruction of justice which has the same effect as perjury and bribery of witnesses must also be a high crime and misdemeanor."

The prosecution also took issue with the president's claims that to remove him on these articles would permanently diminish the presidency and mangle the system of checks and balances:

> Quite the contrary, however, it is President Clinton's behavior as set forth in the articles that has had these effects. Essentially, President Clinton argues that the Presidency and the system of checks and balances can only be saved if we allow the President to commit felonies with impunity. To state that proposition is to refute it. Convicting him and thereby reaffirming that criminal behavior that strikes at the heart of the justice system will result in removal will serve to strengthen the Presidency, not weaken it.

Responding to the president's claim that his conduct was private, the managers argued that "[p]erjury and obstruction of justice as set forth in the articles of impeachment are, by definition, public misconduct":

> Indeed, it is precisely their public nature that makes them offenses—acts that are not crimes when committed outside the judicial realm become crimes when they enter that realm. Lying to one's spouse about an extramarital affair, although immoral, is not a crime. Telling the same lie under oath in a judicial proceeding is a crime. Hiding gifts given to an adulterous lover to conceal the affair, although immoral, is not a crime. When those gifts become potential evidence in a judicial proceeding, the same act becomes a crime. One who has committed these kinds of crimes that corrupt the judicial system simply is not fit to serve as the nation's chief law

Charles Ruff, lead counsel for the president, told senators that the president was innocent of a "witches' brew of charges" brought by the House managers.

enforcement officer. Apart from that, the notion that high crimes and misdemeanors encompass only public misconduct will not bear scrutiny. Numerous "private" crimes would obviously require the removal of a President. For example, if he killed his wife in a domestic dispute or molested a child, no one would seriously argue that he could not be removed. All of these acts violate the President's unique responsibility to take care that the laws be faithfully executed.

The House managers claimed that the standard for impeachment and removal of a president is the same as for a federal judge, that the "argument that Presidents are held to a lower standard of behavior than federal judges completely misreads the Constitution and the Senate's precedents":

> The Constitution provides one standard for the impeachment, conviction, and removal from office. . . . President Clinton argues that the standard differs

because judges have life tenure whereas Presidents are accountable to the voters at elections. That argument fails on several grounds. . . . If electoral accountability were a sufficient means of remedying presidential misconduct, the framers would not have explicitly included the President in the impeachment clause. Finally, even if this argument were otherwise valid, it does not apply to President Clinton because he will never face the voters again. . . . As the person who ultimately directs the Justice Department—the federal government's prosecutorial authority—the President must follow his constitutional duty to take care that the laws are faithfully executed. . . . His special constitutional duty is at least as high, if not higher, than the judge's.

The managers also suggested that:

The 25th Amendment to the Constitution ensures that impeachment and removal of a President would not overturn an election because it is the elected Vice President who would replace the President not the losing presidential candidate. . . . President Clinton argues that the evidence should be tested by the most stringent standard because "there is no suggestion of corruption or misuse of office—or any other conduct that places our system of government at risk in the two remaining years of the President's term. . . ." While the President might be expected to argue that he did not act corruptly, he cannot credibly assert that "there is no suggestion of corruption," because "corrupt" conduct is precisely what he is charged with in the articles of impeachment.

The Senate began hearing the House managers' factual presentation on January 15, 1999. After closing arguments the next day, the president's attorneys presented their defense and closing statements. On January 22, senators submitted written questions to the parties in a question-and-answer session. On January 25, the Senate voted 57-43 against opening its deliberations to the public.

Two days later, on January 27, the Senate voted 56-44 not to dismiss the charges against President Clinton. (Only Democrat Russell Feingold of Wisconsin crossed party lines, voting to proceed with the trial.) Although a 12-person majority had voted to continue, many commentators—and indeed, some senators—observed that the impeachment trial was for all intents and purposes now over. After hearing the factual presentation of the House managers, 44 senators believed there was no basis to continue the trial; obtaining 67 votes to convict—the constitutionally mandated two-thirds majority—would be virtually impossible.

Nevertheless, the Senate also voted on January 27 to permit witness testimony. However, faced with the possibility of extending the impeachment trial by weeks or even months, the Senate decided to limit the number of witnesses the House managers could call to three, and rather than appearing live before the Senate these witnesses would give videotaped depositions.

The House managers chose to depose Monica Lewinsky, Vernon Jordan, and, in a move that surprised many observers, Clinton aide Sidney Blumenthal (to whom Clinton had denied his affair with Lewinsky and declared that it was she who had pursued him). Ultimately, however, the videotaped depositions, excerpts of which the House managers played for the senators, contained no major revelations.

On February 12, 1999, the Senate voted 55-45 to acquit President Clinton on the first article, perjury before a grand jury. Ten Republican senators joined all 45 Democrats in voting for acquittal. On the second article, obstruction of justice, five Republicans voted with the Democrats for acquittal, producing a 50-50 split. Not only had neither article of impeachment garnered a two-thirds majority, neither had won even a simple majority.

"It is therefore ordered and adjudged," Chief Justice Rehnquist announced, "that the said William Jefferson Clinton be, and he hereby is, acquitted of the charges in the said articles." The impeachment process was now officially over.

THE CLINTON IMPEACHMENT IN PERSPECTIVE

In the aftermath of the historic Senate proceedings, politicians and commentators tried to sum up the significance of President Clinton's acquittal. A popular interpretation, especially among Democratic supporters of the president, was that the Constitution had been vindicated. "Let us all understand," Vice President Al Gore declared, "that today's vote—rather than being a victory for any person or party—is instead a reaffirmation of the wisdom of our founders and their design of our Constitution."

Senator Jack Reed of Rhode Island sounded a similar theme. "Today is the culmination of a long and arduous road," he said, "but the Constitution endures. It's stronger than political faction, it's stronger than [the] frailties of any individual, it's as strong as [the] American people."

The American people, polls showed, had heavily favored Clinton's acquittal. Interestingly, polls also showed that a majority of Americans believed Clinton had lied under oath. Indeed, it was difficult even for supporters to believe that some of his statements—for example, that he couldn't recall being alone with Monica Lewinsky—had been anything but out-and-out lies.

Given the circumstances, then, there were those who saw Clinton's acquittal by the Senate as something less than a great day for the Constitution. After all, perjury has always been regarded as a serious offense that undermines the justice system. As early as 1792, John Jay, the first chief justice of the United States, had firmly stated the case against perjury:

> Independent of the abominable Insult which Perjury offers to the divine Being, there is no Crime more extensively pernicious to Society. It discolours and poisons the Streams of Justice, and by substituting Falsehood for Truth, saps the Foundations of personal and public Rights—Controversies of various kinds exist at all Times, and in all Communities. To decide them, Courts of Justice are instituted—their Decisions must be regulated by Evidence, and the greater part of Evidence will always consist of the Testimony of witnesses. This Testimony is given under those solemn obligations which an appeal to the God of Truth impose; and if oaths should cease to be held sacred, our dearest and most valuable Rights would become insecure.

More recently—at a House Judiciary Committee hearing on the background and history of impeachment—Judge Griffin Bell observed, "Truth and fairness are the two essential elements in a justice system. . . . If we don't have truth in the judicial process and in the court system in our country, we don't have anything. We don't have a system." Bell, who was appointed to the federal bench by President John F. Kennedy and served as U.S. attorney general under President Jimmy Carter, also observed: "A President cannot faithfully execute the laws if he himself is breaking them. The statutes against perjury, obstruction of justice and witness tampering rest on vouchsafing the element of truth in judicial proceedings—civil and criminal—and particularly in the grand jury."

Why, then, did the senators vote to acquit? Of perhaps more importance, why didn't they at least permit live testimony, to resolve the conflicting versions of the facts presented by the House managers and the president's defense team? Did the senators shirk their constitutional responsibility to give the charges a full hearing and, as House manager Stephen Buyer claimed, fail to "follow through on their conscience and conviction"? Or did the senators consider the evidence against Clinton and find the evidence lacking— or in the alternative, find that removal was too strong a penalty for the president's alleged behavior?

The Framers' system, while designed to minimize the effect of political passions on impeachment outcomes, relies upon politicians—not judges—to evaluate the merits of impeachment and removal. And politicians are not immune to public opinion. President Clinton was a popular leader presiding over a booming economy in peacetime. Opinion polls repeatedly

At the Andrew Johnson Historical Site in Greeneville, Tennessee, Senator Bill Frist compares admission tickets from the nation's only presidential impeachment trials. Whatever their underlying merits, both the Johnson and Clinton cases confirmed the Founding Fathers' assumption that partisan politics would play a role in the impeachment process.

showed that Americans were tired of the Lewinsky scandal, wanted the matter resolved quickly, and didn't believe that Clinton should be removed from office. Moreover, many people blamed Republicans for conducting what was seen as a politically motivated vendetta against the president.

One interpretation of Clinton's acquittal is that members of both parties weighed the situation and did what was in their political self-interest. According to this interpretation, Senate Democrats supported the leader of their party unwaveringly because they knew public opinion was on his side. Republicans, on the other hand, recognized that they would likely be blamed for a prolonged and partisan impeachment battle, and they had little hope of winning that battle anyway. So they consented to rules (such as the three-witness limit and the barring of live testimony) that cut short the trial and eliminated any chance that new revelations would emerge that might alter the political equation.

While the political dimensions of the Senate trial are undeniable, politics alone may not fully explain President Clinton's acquittal. Like many ordinary Americans, many senators voiced serious concerns about the process by which Clinton had been investigated and ultimately impeached. Senator Charles Schumer of New York expressed a commonly held view when he said, "What happened was that a while ago, a group of people who very much disliked Bill Clinton decided that they would expose his private life, put him through a legal process and try to remove him."

Of course, there is another interpretation—that Clinton, through his unseemly and improper behavior, brought his impeachment troubles upon himself. Nevertheless, Paula Jones's legal effort—whatever the truth or falsity of her allegations against Clinton—had indeed been championed and funded by "people who very much disliked" the president, including right-wing groups such as the Conservative Political Action Con-

ference and the Rutherford Institute. And Kenneth Starr's four-year OIC investigation may have been within the legal bounds of the Independent Counsel Statute, but his tactics often seemed excessive and overzealous—as when OIC investigators tried to pressure Monica Lewinsky into wearing a wire in order to catch the president in an illicit encounter. To senators like Charles Schumer, the possibility that endless partisan investigations might become the norm in American politics seemed more of a danger than did failing to remove Clinton from office for offenses stemming from his attempt to conceal a sexual affair.

Still, many legal scholars expressed concern that illegal conduct on the part of the president had ultimately been excused. And many did not accept the distinction between private behavior and public behavior that Clinton supporters put forward. The sexual affair with Monica Lewinsky may have been private behavior, but the Jones lawsuit brought the matter squarely into the public realm, and at that point the president

Attorneys Robert Bennett (left) and Nathan Lewin, both of whom represented clients targeted by independent counsels, testify at hearings on the Independent Counsel Act held by the Senate Governmental Affairs Committee, March 3, 1999. Ultimately Congress declined to reauthorize the act.

no longer had the option of concealing the affair. Plus, the offenses of which Clinton stood accused seem to fall within the Framers' understanding of what constitutes impeachable conduct.

With opinions thus divided on the merits of the case against Bill Clinton, what conclusions might one draw about the events of 1998 and 1999? Did the impeachment system work as the Framers envisioned? One possible conclusion is that a popular president will be somewhat insulated from the threat of removal and may in fact be held less accountable for his behavior than a president who doesn't enjoy great public support. Joan Hoff, director of the Contemporary History Institute at Ohio State University, has been more categorical in her assessment. Clinton's acquittal, she stated on *The NewsHour with Jim Lehrer*, showed that "you can't impeach a popular president when you're governing through poll-driven forms of government." Furthermore, as long as the numbers of Democrats and Republicans in Congress—and in particular, the Senate—remain fairly even, a loss of support among the president's own party will be necessary to effect his removal. This is not necessarily something the Framers would find troubling, for they wanted to limit partisanship in the impeachment process. As constitutional scholar Raoul Berger observed, "[I]mpeachment of the president should be a last resort. . . . Because it has proven itself infected with the taint of party, it needs to be limited to a cause that would win the assent of 'all right-thinking men,' not merely of an exasperated majority."

In the end, however, the significance of the Clinton case may lie less with what it says about the impeachment process than with what it implies for American politics and the power of the presidency. In the many months leading up to the actual impeachment and trial, decisions made in the courts, the Office of Independent Counsel, and the White House set precedents that may prove difficult for future presidents.

On December 28, 1994, Judge Susan Webber Wright ruled that Paula Jones's lawsuit should be delayed until after Clinton left office, although pretrial fact-finding could proceed. After Jones's lawyers appealed, an appellate court reversed Wright's ruling, and on May 27, 1997, the Supreme Court unanimously agreed with the appellate decision. In the scandal-poisoned climate of contemporary American politics, might this precedent lead to politically inspired lawsuits designed to harass a president?

Another legacy of the Clinton case may be a somewhat diminished presidency. When Kenneth Starr subpoenaed White House aides Bruce Lindsey and Sidney Blumenthal to testify before the grand jury, Clinton sought to limit the scope of the questioning by invoking executive privilege. Executive privilege is a traditionally respected—but not legally mandated—protection from forced disclosure of communications that have taken place within the executive branch of government. The rationale is that to be honest and effective advisers, a president's aides must be confident that they won't later be compelled to divulge what they have said. Starr refused to accept the claim of executive privilege in his criminal investigation, however, and once again the courts ruled against the White House. Along similar lines, a federal appeals court ruled that the testimony of Lindsey, a government lawyer, was not protected by attorney-client privilege; only the president's communications with his private lawyer, the court ruled, should receive that special status. The decision raised the possibility, Clinton supporters argued, that future presidents would be hampered by the need to frequently consult two sets of lawyers.

Starr's OIC also subpoenaed Secret Service agents to testify before the grand jury. Once again, the White House objected, asserting a hitherto unheard-of privilege that, the president's attorneys said, shielded Secret

What lasting effects, if any, the impeachment of Bill Clinton will have upon the powers of the presidency remains to be seen.

Service agents from being forced to testify about what they saw or heard in the course of protecting the president. Clinton—along with former president George Bush and others—argued that the safety of future presidents might be compromised if presidents felt compelled to keep the Secret Service agents assigned to protect them at arm's length for fear they might later be required to testify in legal proceedings. But the OIC rejected this argument, saying that only a president involved in illegal activities would need fear Secret Service testimony. And once again, the matter was litigated, with the courts coming down on the side of Starr and his prosecutors.

In the days and weeks following Clinton's acquittal, historians and political commentators offered various opinions about how the office of the president would be affected. Some predicted a succession of weaker presidents and stronger, more assertive Congresses. Others believed that this would not necessarily happen, because the strength of the presidency is so connected with the qualities of the person who currently occupies the office. Just as, for example, the presidency had been weakened considerably under Herbert Hoover but rebounded under his successor, Franklin D. Roosevelt, so might an extraordinary chief executive reinvigorate the office after Clinton's departure. Many commentators, however, did predict increased cynicism and distrust of government, along with a continuing decline in voter participation.

One clear casualty of the Clinton impeachment was the Independent Counsel Act, which had played such a large role in shaping events. The act had always had critics who contended that giving special prosecutors virtually unlimited time, money, and discretion to expand their original investigations often made for legal "fishing" expeditions, and even when no wrong-doing was discovered targets of these investigations ran up huge legal bills and suffered damaged reputations. The uncommon tenacity (critics would say overzeal-ousness) of Starr's OIC investigation spelled the end of the controversial statute, which Congress declined to reauthorize in 1999. Ironically, one of those arguing for the end of the statute was Kenneth Starr himself.

As for Starr's nemesis, Bill Clinton, the acquittal on impeachment charges in the Senate did not spell the end of his legal setbacks. On April 12, 1999, Judge Susan Webber Wright issued a ruling holding the president in contempt for his testimony in the Jones deposition, which she characterized as "false, misleading and evasive." It was the first time a sitting president had been held in contempt of court. Judge Wright eventually fined the president $90,686. "[S]anctions must be imposed," she explained, "to redress the President's misconduct and to deter others who might consider emulating the President's misconduct."

Bibliography

Berger, Raoul. *Impeachment: The Constitutional Problems*. Cambridge, Mass.: Harvard University Press, 1974.

Black, Charles L. *Impeachment: A Handbook*. New Haven, Conn.: Yale University Press, 1974.

Blackstone, William. *Commentaries on the Laws of England*, 4 vols. Oxford: Clarendon Press, 1778.

Cooke, Jacob E., ed. *The Federalist*. Middletown, Conn.: Wesleyan University Press, 1961.

Coulter, Ann. *High Crimes and Misdemeanors*. Washington, D.C.: Regnery, 1998.

Curtis, George Ticknor, *History of the Origin, Formation, and Adoption of the Constitution of the United States: With Notices of Its Principal Framers*. New York: Harper, 1854–1860.

Farrand, Max, ed. *Records of the Federal Convention of 1787*. 4 vols. New Haven, Conn.: Yale University Press, 1936.

Hoffer, Peter Charles, and N. E. H. Hull. *Impeachment in America, 1635–1805*. New Haven, Conn.: Yale University Press, 1984.

Holdsworth, William S. *History of English Law*. 17 vols. London: Metheun, 1903–1966.

Rehnquist, William H. *Grand Inquests*. New York: William Morrow, 1992.

Smith, James M., and Paul L. Murphy, eds. *Liberty and Justice*. 2 vols. New York: Knopf, 1965.

Story, Joseph. *Commentaries on the Constitution of the United States: With a Preliminary Review of the Constitutional History of the Colonies and States, Before the Adoption of the Constitution*. 2nd ed. Boston: C. C. Little and J. Brown, 1851.

Warren, Charles. *The Making of the Constitution*. Boston: Little, Brown, 1928.

Index

Adams, John, 60
Albright, Madeleine, 33
American Revolution, 25, 55
Anti-Federalists, 26-27
Arkansas, 13, 15, 16

Bell, Griffin, 100
Bennett, Robert, 21, 22-23, 39-41, 87
Berger, Raoul, 104
Bill of Rights, 60
Black's Law Dictionary, 83
Blackstone, William, 51, 52, 54, 81-82
Blennerhassett, Harman, 63
Blumenthal, Sidney, 97, 105
Bribery, 51, 52, 65, 91
Buchanan, James, 69
Burr, Aaron, 63-64
Bush, George, 106
Buyer, Stephen, 101

Carter, Jimmy, 100
Castle Grande, 16
Chase, Samuel, 59-63, 64, 67
Civil rights lawsuits, 13, 15, 20, 40, 78
Civil War, 65, 68, 69
Clinton, Hillary, 16
Clinton, William Jefferson
    acquittal of, 97, 99-103, 107
    defense of, 86-93
    grand jury testimony of, 38-43, 65, 80, 86-87, 97
    impeachment of, 75-97, 99

    and Lewinsky scandal, 19-21, 31-44, 88-90, 100, 102
    and Paula Jones case, 13-16, 18-19, 20, 21-23, 31, 35, 39-41, 42, 43, 44, 77, 79, 80, 86-90, 102-3, 105
    and Whitewater, 16-18
Commentaries on the Laws of England (Blackstone), 51, 53
Common law, 51, 62
Confederate States of America, 65, 68
Congress, U.S., 16, 18, 41, 61, 68, 69, 71, 75, 80, 104, 107. *See also* House of Representatives, U.S.; Senate, U.S.
Conservative Political Action Conference, 102-3
Constitution, U.S.
    and impeachment, 25-29, 47-57, 60, 72, 81, 94-96, 99, 100
    and treason, 51-52, 54, 64, 91
Constitutional Convention, 25-29, 47-57
Contemporary History Institute at Ohio State University, 104
Crittendon-Johnson Resolution, 68
Currie, Betty, 35-36, 41, 77, 89, 90

Daley, William, 33

Daschle, Tom, 86
Davie, William R., 27-28
Declaration of Independence, 25, 60
Discovery (legal process), 14-15, 35, 79
Dixon, James, 73
DNA evidence, 38-39
Double jeopardy, 57-58

Emory, William, 71, 72
England, 51, 54-56
Equal Employment Opportunity Commission, 14
Executive privilege, 41, 105

FBI files scandal, 18
Federalists, 26
Feingold, Russell, 96
Fessenden, William Pitt, 73
First Continental Congress, 60
Fiske, Robert, 17-18
Foster, Vincent, 18
Franklin, Benjamin, 25, 28

Gerry, Elbridge, 28
Gore, Al, 99
Grand Inquests (Rehnquist), 63, 64, 71

Hamilton, Alexander, 25, 53
Hastings, Alcee, 65
Hastings, Warren, 55
Hay, George, 64
Hoff, Joan, 104
Holdsworth, William S., 56
Hoover, Herbert, 107
House managers, 85, 86, 92, 93, 94-96, 97, 101

Index

JUSTIN FERNANDEZ, a native of Newark, New Jersey, and a licensed attorney in Ohio, is a graduate of the University of Cincinnati College of Law; a former law clerk for the Ohio Court of Appeals, Second Appellate District; and a former legal editor for Anderson Publishing Company, Cincinnati, Ohio. Mr. Fernandez, founder and director of the Agency for the Digital & Literary Arts, Inc., a business-to-business literary and intellectual property agency, has been a literary agent since 1995 and is also active in sports agenting through a joint venture with Pro Sports Ltd., in Beverly Hills, California.

AUSTIN SARAT is William Nelson Cromwell Professor of Jurisprudence and Political Science at Amherst College, where he also chairs the Department of Law, Jurisprudence and Social Thought. Professor Sarat is the author or editor of 23 books and numerous scholarly articles. Among his books are *Law's Violence, Sitting in Judgment: Sentencing the White Collar Criminal,* and *Justice and Injustice in Law and Legal Theory.* He has received many academic awards and held several prestigious fellowships. He is President of the Law & Society Association and Chair of the Working Group on Law, Culture and the Humanities. In addition, he is a nationally recognized teacher and educator whose teaching has been featured in the *New York Times,* on the *Today* show, and on National Public Radio's *Fresh Air.*

Picture Credits

SEA STAR
ORPHAN OF CHINCOTEAGUE

SEA STAR

ORPHAN OF CHINCOTEAGUE

By MARGUERITE HENRY

Illustrated by Wesley Dennis

MACMILLAN PUBLISHING COMPANY
NEW YORK

To

IRVING JACOBY

CONTENTS

LAST PONY PENNING, I went to Chincoteague a second time. My purpose was to work with the movie men who were planning to film the book of *Misty*. I had no thought of writing another Chincoteague story. *Misty*, I thought, was complete in itself. Let the boys and girls dream their own wonderful sequels.

And then all my resolves burst in midair. Early on the morning after Pony Penning, a lone colt with a crooked star on his forehead was found at Tom's Cove. His mamma "lay on her broadside, dead."

Except for the sea mews and the striker birds, the colt was quite alone, one little wild thing, helpless against the wild sea.

And there, in that wild moment at Tom's Cove, the story of Sea Star was born of itself.

M. H.

SEA STAR
ORPHAN OF CHINCOTEAGUE

Chapter 1

BRAIDS AND RIBBONS

PAUL WAS separating each silver hair in Misty's tail. At his feet lay a little pile of blackberry brambles which he had removed, one by one.

With an air of secrecy he looked around quickly to make sure no outsider could overhear what he was about to say. But he and his sister, Maureen, were quite alone in the barnyard of Pony Ranch — except for the wild fowl and the ponies. There was no need at all to whisper, but Paul did whisper, and he seemed to be laughing at a private little joke of his own.

"How'd you like to see Misty's tail braided?"

"Braided!" Maureen dropped the gunny sack with which she was brushing Misty's coat and stared. "How silly! Who-ever heard of a wild Chincoteague pony with a braided tail!"

"Nobody except you and me." Paul looked around again, chuckling to himself. "Nobody'll ever know except the guinea hens and ducks and geese, and who listens to them?"

Surprise crept into Maureen's voice. "How'd you guess, Paul?"

"Guess what?"

"That I've been hankering to do Misty up like those pic-tures we saw in the paper, the ones of the horses at the big show?"

Paul laid the comb he had been using on Misty's rump.

"Mental telegraphy, of course. Miss Vic says when two people think the same thing it's mental telegraphy."

"She does?"

"Yes. And I believe it!" Paul's voice no longer whispered. It chortled in amusement. "For two nights now I've been dream-ing Misty was a famous steeplechaser, and we had to braid her tail and mane and trim off her fetlocks and whiskers and clean her coat until if you patted her hip you couldn't raise a single puff of dust. Not a puff."

Maureen dipped a corner of the gunny sack in a pail of water and began scrubbing Misty's knees.

Her words came jerking out to the motion of the scrubbing. "We'll tie her braids with fancy ribbons. We'll put a wreath of flowers round her neck—like Grandpa says they do at the big races over on the main."

14

Paul giggled. "Grandpa'd say we're chuckleheads, but let's do it, anyway! Then we'll take pictures in our mind, and afore anyone else sees her we'll shake out her tail and her mane and let the wind rumple 'em all up so she looks exactly like a Chincoteague pony again."

Though scores of ponies came and went on Grandpa Beebe's Pony Ranch, Misty stayed. For she belonged to Paul and Maureen. They talked to her as if she were human, and often it seemed that she talked back! Now, as if she understood their plans, she spun around, kicked the comb from her back, burst through the unfastened rope fence, and headed for the marshland, her mane tossing in the sea breeze.

Disturbed by her motion, the barnyard went wild with noise. Guinea hens, geese, ducks — wild ones and tame ones flew into the air with a great clatter. A bunch of ponies in the corral who, a moment before, had been dozing in the sun, alerted and were off, following the silver direction-flag of Misty's tail.

"My stars!" laughed Maureen. "That Misty's got the sharpest ears and the knowingest mind of any pony I ever did see. Look at her. She's gone wild as her mother—bucking and leaping and kicking her heels at our plan."

Watching Misty, Paul and Maureen thought a moment of her mother, the famous wild Phantom on near-by Assateague Island. Then Paul said, "But Misty is not really wild; in two minutes she'll be back, asking for those braids and ribbons."

Maureen did quick little capers of her own, mimicking Misty. She stumbled over the pail, spilling out half of the water before she rescued it. "Look at her!" she said, a little out of breath. "She's the same color as the flowers of the kinks bush. And she floats on the wind, like they do." A note of anxiety showed in her voice as she went on. "You think the other ponies get jealous of Misty?"

"'Course not. They don't ever get jealous of a leader. Grandpa says it's the first time he's seen a mare colt to be the leader."

They watched the older ponies trying to follow Misty's antics. The more Misty galloped and bucked and twisted her body into the air, the more Paul's and Maureen's laughter rippled out over the marshland of Chincoteague Island.

16

"The big ones are clumsy as woods cows beside our Misty!"
Maureen said.

Now Paul threw his head back and let out a shrill whistle. It was as if he had roped Misty with his voice. She jammed to a halt. Her head and tail went up. Then she wheeled and came flying in, the rest of the band stringing out behind her.

Maureen and Paul ran for the gate. When the entire bunch was safely inside, they fastened it securely.

Misty flew on past them to the entrance of her stall. There she settled down to earth like a bird after flight. She watched the other ponies go to a big open shed which they shared. Then she stood waiting at her manger, waiting for the little reward of corn and the pleasant scratchy feeling of the gunny sack.

Maureen went back to work, this time on Misty's muddy hocks. "We got to hurry, Paul," she said, "before Grandpa gets back from Watson Town. I promised him I'd do Grandma's work today."

Paul did not answer Maureen. His words were for Misty's furry ears. "You're fierce and wild and wonderful when you come in all blown, your nose snortin' white flames like a dragon. I wonder if even Man o' War could have been as exciting looking."

Maureen stopped scrubbing and stood up in thought. "No, Paul," she said slowly. "I reckon even Man o' War didn't have as much fire."

Misty, impatient with all the talk, moved over to a wash tub that was turned upside down and placed her forefeet on it. "Here, you!" she seemed to say. "Do I have to do *all* my tricks for a few kernels of corn?"

She lifted a forefoot high, pawing the air.

Paul caught it and shook it vigorously. "How do, Misty," he said, bowing very gravely. "I failed to see you in church last Sunday. Hope you weren't ailing."

Misty lipped Paul's straw-like hair to see if there was any taste to it. Finding none, she nudged his head out of the way and reached for the niblets of corn that he now produced from his pocket.

From all over the farmyard chickens and hens came running, pecking up the little kernels Misty dropped.

"Now she's clean and had a good run; so we can ready her for the show," Paul said. "That is, if you can find any ribbons."

Maureen was in and out of the weathered house beyond the corral before Paul had three strands of forelock ready to braid.

"Here's lots of ribbons," she called. "They came tied around Grandma's presents when she was in the hospital. She brought them home for me to do my hair, but I've been saving them up for Misty." She spread them out on the up-turned wash tub. "Let's use all different colors."

Misty liked the attention she was getting. She preferred the company of humans to that of the other ponies. They tried to sneak her ear corn, and nose into her water barrel. But the boy and the girl—they neither snatched her food nor drank her water. They brought it instead!

She nipped their clothes playfully as the friendly, awkward hands braided and looped her mane and forelock.

"My fingers get all twisted," Paul complained, "but if stable boys over on the main can do it, so can I."

"Why, your braids look better than mine, Paul. You've looped yours underneath instead of over on top. But my bows are tied better, I think. Now let's do her tail."

Misty snatched little colt naps as they worked on her tail. A fresh wind from the sea fanned her face. It fluttered the ribbons on her forelock and mane. Every little while she would shake her head and make the braids dance. Then she would give a high horselaugh into the pleasant July morning.

20

When the tail was tied in red and pink and blue ribbons, Maureen went off to gather an armful of flowers from the patch of Bouncing Bess at the side of the house. The stems were thick and strong, and she braided them so that the flower heads came close together, making a huge pink wreath.

"It's funny," she thought to herself, "I've done this often in my mind. The Bouncing Bess. Grandma's ribbons. The skinny little braids. It's as if we'd planned it all out together."

On the way back, she tried the wreath around her own neck.

"Prettier than a wreath of roses, don't you think, Paul?"

"Bigger, anyway," he said.

Together they placed the flowers around Misty's neck. Then they stood back, running their eyes over the picture before them—the wreath hanging down almost to Misty's knees, the tiny silver braids with dozens of gaily colored bows.

Paul grinned broadly, both a little ashamed and a little proud of his handiwork. "Jumpin' grasshoppers! No one would know her from a blue ribbon winner. Why, her pedigree is busting out all over!" He half-closed his eyes, reciting, "Misty —out of the Phantom by the Pied Piper."

"Who before that?"

"Pied Piper out of the Wild Wind by the Wild Waves . . . Out of . . ."

Maureen's laughter bubbled. "We haven't got time to go all the way back to the ponies that swam ashore from the wrecked galleon. Come on! Let's make believe I'm the man who leads the winner before the grandstand, and you're the jockey."

A handful of ribbon lay at Paul's feet. Quickly he picked out a wide band of purple satin and fastened it across his shirt like a jockey. Then he climbed up close to Misty's withers so he would not be too heavy for her. He bowed to the imaginary crowds, bowed again and again, as Maureen led Misty around

22

the corral. Now he was accepting the imaginary silver cup while the people went mad with applause. He closed his eyes, listening to the sound of it. It was deafening. It roared and roared in his ears until they hurt.

"Paul! Paul!" Maureen shouted above the noise. "Open your eyes. It's a plane. Heading toward us. It's going to land. Paul! Right here at Pony Ranch!"

Chapter 2

THE SILVER PLANE

PAUL STARTED from his daydreams. Misty was trembling under him, prancing in fear. He slid off and blindfolded her with his hands. The spear of light in the sky was a silver plane. It came darting in, landing down meadow, taxiing toward them.

As it settled to a stop, three men scrambled out. One stayed with the plane. The other two came walking toward Pony Ranch, looking around and about them like men who had suddenly landed from Mars.

Maureen gazed awestruck. "Reckon something's the matter of their engine?" she asked.

Paul looked and gave a nod. "Or maybe they meant to land at the Government base on the other side of the island." He turned Misty loose and started for the plane at a dead run. Maureen was close at his heels.

Now that the whirring monster was still, Misty was full of curiosity, too. Ears pricked forward, she jog-trotted alongside Paul and Maureen, the wreath bobbing against her chest. The other ponies followed at a cautious distance, but when they reached the gate, Misty drove them back. Then she rejoined the boy and girl.

"It's like history," Paul said as he ran. "Columbus and his party lands and the natives go out to meet them."

Maureen laughed nervously, "They don't look to me like faraway people."

Now the two men and the boy and girl were close enough to study each other. Uncertainly they all stopped in their tracks and stood very still on the narrow spit of land. In the sudden quiet the sound of rustling grasses and channel waves skipping into shore grew loud and distinct.

Paul and Maureen waited, listening.

"Good morning," said one of the men, with a smile as warming as sunlight.

"How do," nodded Paul and Maureen solemnly.

The man who had spoken was low-voiced, and his blue eyes were very young and very old. The look he gave them was not the look a grownup gives to boys and girls, but one that friends save for each other. "My name is Van Meter," he said, "and this is my associate, Mr. Jacobs."

Mr. Jacobs was a tall man, and his eyes were dark and deep like the sheltering coolness of a pine grove. "How do," he said, repeating Paul's and Maureen's way of greeting

Misty broke the awkward pause that followed. A bug flew into her nose and she snorted it out so fiercely that her braided forelock flew straight up.

They all laughed and the strangeness was gone.

"This must be Pony Ranch," said Mr. Jacobs, looking at the fences and sheds as if he carried a blueprint of them in his mind.

"It is!" exclaimed Maureen.

"And you must be Paul and Maureen Beebe."

The boy and girl nodded in wide-eyed amazement.

"But this pony," said Mr. Van Meter, his eyes taking in the wreath of Bouncing Bess and the braids and ribbons, "it can't be! No, it can't possibly be—Misty!"

Paul picked up a piece of marsh grass and twiddled it between his fingers. "It *is* Misty," he said, embarrassed by the silly ribbons and wreath.

Mr. Van Meter was plainly disappointed. As he turned his head he caught a glimpse of a little herd of wild ponies frisking along the beach of neighboring Assateague Island. He gestured toward the wind-blown creatures. "I expected to find Misty with her mane and tail blowing in the wind," he said, talking more to himself than to the others. "And I hoped she'd have some of the mystery of the sea in her look."

"Oh, but she does!" exclaimed Paul and Maureen together. Quickly they lifted the wreath of flowers from her neck and began loosening her braids.

Maureen glanced up shyly as she worked, "We just wanted to see how she'd look if she won a big race over on the main."

"And how *do* you think she looks?" asked Mr. Jacobs.

The boy and girl were shaking out the strands of hair.

"You say, Maureen."

"No, you, Paul. Do you like Misty all prissied up with ribbons and things?"

Paul answered easily. "Even before we started, we knew we'd like her better with her mane and tail free."

"Good! So do I." Mr. Van Meter smiled with his eyes. "Now, will you take us to meet your Grandpa Beebe?"

"He's gone up the island to Watson Town. Grandma's been having trouble with her biddies, and he wanted to talk to Miss Vic about them."

"Oh."

"He sometimes gets hung up talking," explained Maureen, "but nearly always he comes back pretty quick."

"Perhaps," suggested Mr. Jacobs, "we could talk to Mrs. Beebe until he gets back."

Paul shook his head. "She's gone to Richmond with Clarence Lee."

"Yes," added Maureen proudly. "Our uncle, Clarence Lee, Jr., is going to go to college. He may learn so much he could be a preacher!"

The strangers seemed to be turning matters over in their minds. There was a little pause before they spoke. "Perhaps you would like to hear our mission," Mr. Van Meter finally said.

"Oh!" Maureen looked surprised. "Are you missionaries?"

Paul snorted. " 'Course not, Maureen. Whenever are you going to grow up? Mr. Van Meter means that maybe we'd like to know why they came to our island. And how they know all about us and Misty," he added.

Maureen blushed. "Please to come and sit down on the benches underneath the pine trees," she invited politely.

Together they walked over to the pine grove at the side of the house while Misty, free of her wreath and halter, kicked up her heels and trotted off to sniff and snort at the strange silver bird resting on her private exercise ground.

The two men watched her with a pleased expression. Then Mr. Van Meter took a snapshot out of his billfold and passed it to Paul and Maureen. "These are my two children," he said. "Last Christmas they were given a book that told the legend of a Spanish galleon wrecked long ago in a storm, and how her cargo of Moor ponies swam ashore to Assateague Island, and how descendants of those ponies are living wild and free on the island today."

Paul and Maureen looked up from the picture. "That's just how it happened," said Maureen.

"Don't talk, Maureen. Listen. Listen to what's coming. Maybe it's going to be something good."

"It *is* good," Mr. Van Meter went on. "My boy and girl kept telling me about the roundup of the wild ponies you people of Chincoteague have every year."

"It's this week!" Paul blurted out.

Mr. Van Meter nodded as if he knew all about it. "Finally I got as excited as my children, so excited that I talked it all over with Mr. Jacobs. We want to make a movie of it."

Paul and Maureen just stared. They could scarcely believe their ears. A movie made about the wild ponies of Assateague! Then Maureen became thoughtful. "Would Misty be in it?" she asked. "She was born on Assateague, but she's not wild any more."

"That's why we are here. We'd like to use the real Misty in the picture, the little colt that was in the book."

Now Maureen clapped her hands for joy and Paul leaped to his feet, letting out his shrill whistle. Misty came flying in, asking questions with her ears. He whispered the good news to her, laughing to see her ears swivel this way and that, as if to catch every word he was saying. Then she was off again, circling the plane and browsing all around it as if she were afraid it might eat her grass.

"We knew you'd like it," said Mr. Van Meter. "That's what we came to see your Grandpa about. We want to buy Misty."

"Buy her!" Two heads jerked up as if they were on puppet strings.

"Yes, we'd like to take her back to New York in that plane — on Friday after Pony Penning. You see," he explained, "the roundup scenes over on Assateague and the swim of the ponies across the channel we want to make down here. But all the close-up scenes could be done better in our studio in New York. It will take months, because colts can't work long at a stretch."

"But why," Paul cried, "why would you have to *buy* her?"

"Because," Mr. Van Meter said soberly, "we'd want to keep her a while after the screen play is made. We'd want to take her to schools and libraries where boys and girls could meet her. We'd want to fix a stall for her in the theaters where her picture was showing so that they could see the real Misty. It might be a long time before she could come back."

"Yes," added Mr. Jacobs, "and you are grownup enough to know that we would have to buy her to carry out our plans. We would have to be responsible for her."

The two men were like jugglers. But instead of balls, they were using words, tossing them back and forth over Maureen's and Paul's heads. Always the words seemed out of reach.

Mr. Van Meter said, "We had a feeling you might want to share Misty with boys and girls everywhere."

"Boys and girls who have never seen a real pony," Mr. Jacobs continued.

It was Mr. Van Meter's turn now. "Sometimes when I

33

hear children in New York talk about Misty, it seems she no longer belongs to a boy and a girl on an island, but to boys and girls everywhere."

The words kept flying, back and forth, higher and higher. "Misty has grown bigger than you know," Mr. Jacobs said. "She isn't just a pony. She's a heroine in a book!"

Paul pounded his fists against the rough hard bark of a pine tree. Maureen turned her back on the men, digging her bare toes in a bed of moss.

"There, now," comforted Mr. Van Meter, "if you do not want to sell her, we will think no less of you."

A silence came over them all. It grew deeper and deeper. Even the hens and chickens stopped scratching, and far down the marshland Misty lay down to sleep.

The sound of a chugging truck was welcome relief.

"That'll be Grandpa," Paul said.

Grandpa Beebe brought the truck to a stop. He got out and squinted down meadow at the silver plane. He took off his battered hat and scratched his head in puzzlement.

"Grandpa! Oh, Grandpa! Come!" Paul and Maureen shouted, panic in their voices.

Grandpa came swinging toward them. "What you two bellerin' about?" he yelled right back at them. "Ye sound like a couple bull calves caught in a bob-wire fence."

"Oh, Grandpa," cried Maureen, throwing herself on him, "they want to make a movie of Misty, and they want to buy her and take her away. Oh, Grandpa!" The words lost themselves in great heaving sobs.

34

Grandpa put Maureen away from him. He strode over to the two men and faced them eye to eye. "If I was a younger fella," he exploded, shaking a gnarled forefinger at them, "I'd give ye more'n a battle of words. Ye should be downright ashamed o' yerselves. Grown men come to hoss trade with childern! Oncet when I was a mere little boy in my nine I went out to Hog Island and I come upon some nestes, fish hawks' nestes they was, and I stole some eggs outen 'em. That night I woke up in the dark and I felt mean and shriveled inside. And that's how you two should feel now."

The men started to speak, but Grandpa waved for silence.

"Why, Paul and Maureen here has raised Misty from a teensy baby. I reckon Misty figgers they're her pappy and mammy." He clapped his hat on his head and looked from one to the other. "Why, Paul here saved Misty from drownding and oncet he stayed a hull night in a truck with her, and him and his sister bought her with their own earned money. You city fellas maybe wouldn't understand, but livin' out here on this lonely marshland, why, Misty's the nighest to a friend these childern got."

"But, Mr. Beebe, we do understand—" Mr. Jacobs started to say more, but Grandpa turned his back and talked to the boy and girl.

"Mind the time Misty got in the chicken swill and et all them green apple peels and got the colic? Mind how we three had to stay up walkin' her and walkin' her all the night long?"

Maureen blew her nose.

"I do, Grandpa," Paul said. "And I recomember last Christmas when we fixed cardboard antlers to Misty's ears and slung two gunny sacks with toys pokin' out of 'em over her back. Recomember?"

"I do!" Maureen spoke up. "And she had holly berries

tucked in her mane and jingle bells tinklin' from her halter."

Grandpa Beebe's voice gentled like a thunderstorm turned into a spring rain. He included the two strangers in the circle now. "Yep," he chuckled. "We took her right smack into the church for the childern's Christmas party. You should of heard the childern laugh to see a pony in church. But one o' 'em spoke

up mighty cute. No bigger than a turnip that kid weren't, and his voice was jest a mouse-squeak, but he come up to Misty an' he said, 'The little Lord Jesus was borned in a stable, and He'd like as not let a pony come to His house.' Then Misty passed the presents around from her packs."

"Stop!" cried Mr. Van Meter. "Can't you see the more you tell us about Misty the more we want her?"

But Paul and Maureen and Grandpa went on as if they had not heard. "Mind the time we brought her into the kitchen," Paul asked Maureen, "and Grandpa was washing his face over by the mirror, and when he looked up there was Misty laughing over his shoulder?"

Grandpa slapped his thigh. "I tell ye, fellas, 'twas the funniest sight I ever see. I looks up at that shaggy face in the mirror and thinks I to myself, 'Great guns, I'm gettin' whiskery!'"

Grandpa cut his laughter short. "What in tunket am I laughin' at? This ain't funny! Now you two strangers tell yer story and be right smart quick about it. Me and Paul got to go down the peninsula today."

Mr. Van Meter looked to Mr. Jacobs and Mr. Jacobs sent the look back. "You tell it, Van. You have children of your own."

Patiently, Mr. Van Meter told the whole story from start to finish. He explained, too, that his company was young and struggling and could afford to pay only two hundred and fifty dollars for Misty. "But," he added quickly, "if the children do not wish to sell her, we shall think no less of them."

"Thar's yer answer, then. We'll help ye all we kin with yer picture-making, but Misty's next to the Bible with us. Why, she's got the map of the United States on her withers, just like her wild mommy, the Phantom."

"And," added Mr. Jacobs very quietly, "the marking on her side is in the shape of a plow, like the state of Virginia."

Grandpa looked surprised. "Call her in, Paul."

Paul let out his shrill summons. It roused Misty from her sleep. She listened for the whistle again. This time it came louder. She thrust her forefeet in front of her, got up sleepily and came lazing in.

Grandpa took hold of her forelock. He turned her around "By smoke!" he exclaimed. "She *has* got the marking of Virginia on her. The shape of a plow it is." He grew tongue-tied for a moment. Then he smiled. "I'm sorry I was snappish and made such a big to-do. But," he added sternly, "the answer is still no."

"Grandpa," suggested Paul, "don't you figure they could find a good colt to buy at the Pony Penning sale after the roundup?"

"'Course you could," Grandpa told the men. "And Paul and Maureen'll help ye all ye want during Pony Penning time. They'll be glad to run yer errands and tell ye where the ponies will be druv, and where they'll be swum acrost the channel. Now we got lots of work to do. Maureen's got to do the cookin' for her Grandma, and me and Paul have got big business down to Cape Charles." He started to walk off. "You two goin' up in that air buggy or could we drop ye off uptown?"

"We'd like a ride to the inn uptown," Mr. Van Meter told Grandpa. "Our pilot friend is anxious to be off for Norfolk as soon as he finds out if we are welcome here."

"Well, ye're welcome to go about yer picture taking, all right. Come along. We'll go down and tell yer friend. Then I'll drop ye off at the inn."

Chapter 3

A MILL DAY

MAUREEN WENT into the house. It was hard to settle down to her chores until the plane was gone. She heard its engines warming, heard it roar down the point of land. She ran to the window to see it take off, blowing the grass into ripples behind it.

Two cameras and a little cluster of luggage were left behind. Paul and Grandpa, Mr. Van Meter and Mr. Jacobs, each picked up a load and carried it to the truck. Now the truck was moving away too, and soon Pony Ranch was bathed in silence.

Maureen put on Grandma Beebe's apron, wrapping it

twice around her and tying it in front. The breakfast dishes were still on the table, beds unmade, rugs rumpled on the floor. She looked around, wrinkling her sunburnt nose. "I'd rather clean out the pony stable and all the chicken coops than clean house!" she thought to herself.

But it was seldom Grandma Beebe left Pony Ranch, and Maureen had promised to take her place. She lighted the flame under a big pot of beans. Then she stood in the middle of the floor thinking.

"I wonder—" she said out loud in the quiet of the house. "No!" she stamped her foot. "No, we couldn't sell Misty. We just couldn't." And she turned briskly to the unmade beds.

Meanwhile, Paul and Grandpa had left the two men at the little frame inn and were driving across the causeway, leaving Chincoteague Island far behind.

All the way down the long peninsula to Cape Charles no mention was made of Mr. Van Meter and Mr. Jacobs. It was almost as if they had never dropped out of the sky at all.

"Mighty nice cabbages in that patch," Grandpa would say. "And the 'taters'll soon be ready to dig, I reckon."

"Uh-hmm," Paul would answer. "How many ponies you figure to sell down to Cape Charles, Grandpa?"

"Oh, a whole flock, likely. Tim Button wants to use 'em to hawk his garden truck through the streets."

"Grandpa?"

"What is it, boy?"

"Why do the people over on the main say *herds* of ponies, and we say *flocks?*"

42

"Why!" thundered Grandpa, taking one hand off the wheel to rub the spiky white whiskers in his ears, "it's 'cause Chincoteague ponies is different, that's why. They fly on the wind like birds. But," snorted Grandpa, "the horses over on the main — they be earthbound critters."

Pleased with the answer, the boy fell silent.

A truck cut in ahead of them. It was packed solidly with dark red tomatoes. Paul counted the crates, guessing at the number of tomatoes in each, then at the total tomatoes in the truck.

The day was slowly raveling itself out. Big Tim Button had changed his mind about wanting to buy the ponies. "Sorry, Beebe," he twanged through his nose, "but I just signed some papers to buy a couple secondhand trucks." And he threw out his chest, slapping the papers in his pocket as if he were not sorry at all.

Tired and discouraged, Grandpa and Paul headed for home. On the way they stopped at the ferry station to pick up Grandma and her friend, Mrs. Tilley, just back from Richmond. Paul had to climb into the body of the truck to make room for them.

He made believe he was a pony being shipped away. He could poke his nose right into the cab because a colt had already done that and broken the glass in the window. Paul looked between the beards of wheat that decorated Grandma's hat and giggled to himself. If he were a pony now, he would rip off the wheat and eat it. Then, like as not, he would trample the hat.

He looked at Grandma to see if she would mind. But her eyes were absently following the fields along the road. He doubted if she would care at all. Mrs. Tilley, however, was lively as a wren, chattering and wagging her head, opening her purse, shutting it again, fussing with her packages. She would fly into a fit if a pony ate her hat. Paul grinned at the thought.

Then he turned his back and sat down quickly to squelch the idea. He dangled his feet over the tailgate and watched the road unroll like a bolt of white ribbon behind them.

It was almost sundown when they turned in at Pony Ranch.

Grandma sniffed audibly as soon as the truck door opened. "Paul! Run into the house, quick. The pot of beans is burning!"

Heavily, she got out and walked up the steps into the house. Maureen met her. "You got the best smellers in the whole world, Grandma! The beans were just fixing to burn, but you saved 'em."

With a kiss and a pat, Grandma whisked off Maureen's apron and tied it around herself. "There!" she sighed, "I'd sooner have bread and molasses and burned beans to home than fine vittles on the main."

At supper that night when Grandpa had finished his plate of beans and spooned up every drop of molasses, he turned to Grandma. "How about yer trip, Ida? How does it feel to have a boy in college?"

"I—don't—know," answered Grandma, with a long pause after each word, "I just don't know."

"Well, where's Clarence Lee, Jr.? Ain't he got hisself all enrolled in that fine school?"

Grandma exchanged a glance with Grandpa, then nodded her head toward Paul and Maureen as if she did not want to discuss the matter in front of them.

"Oh," chuckled Grandpa, "if it's the childern ye're worried about, ye can forget them. They done a heap of growin' up today."

Grandma put down her fork. "I would feel better maybe if I did talk things out," she said, looking from one to the other. "They were mighty nice to me there at the school." She paused, then rushed on. "But the tuition money — it's got to be paid ahead of time. Seems like the school is so overcrowded. There's more young men want to enroll than there's places for 'em to sit down."

"Why can't they bring in stools and folding chairs," interrupted Grandpa, "like we do when the church is full?"

"I spoke of that, but they just smiled at me." Grandma let out a big sigh. "I've had a mill day, Clarence. Seems like my heart's been tromped on. I did so want Clarence Lee to go to college and be a preacher."

"Where's the boy at now?"

"He stayed to Richmond, trying to raise the money. But, Clarence, I'm all worried up. He's got to take some kind of tests and he's trying to earn a pile of money at the same time. Some boys can work hard and study too. But they ain't had the bad pneumonia. Besides, most of them just get the gist of what they're studying. Clarence Lee, now — well, he's got to go deep down."

"Ye say a pile of money, Ida. How much do ye mean, exactly?"

"Three hundred dollars."

"Three hundred dollars!" echoed Grandpa.

"I know, Clarence. The grass was late coming this spring, and ten of your best mares died off. I know. . . . But it was a pitiable sight to see him walk out that door, looking lost and lonely, like a colt cut out from a big bunch of his friends."

"Dang it all!" raged Grandpa. "Ef only Tim Button had taken them ponies. All I got to my name is fifty dollars."

46

Paul and Maureen had long since stopped eating. They looked up from their plates at the same time and suddenly their glances locked. Then, white-faced, they nodded to each other.

"Grandma," Paul spoke very quickly, as if he were afraid he might change his mind, "two movie men were here today. They came to buy Misty."

"For two hundred and fifty dollars," added Maureen.

Grandma's coffee cup was half way to her lips. She set it back down again without touching it.

"You didn't sell her!" she exclaimed, aghast.

"Well, practically," Paul said. "As soon as they give us the money."

"You see, Grandma," Maureen explained very carefully as if she were talking to a little girl, "Misty really doesn't belong just to us any more. She's grown bigger than our island. She's in a book, Grandma. Now she belongs to boys and girls everywhere."

"Yes," Paul's voice warmed. "They want to take her to schools and libraries for children to meet—children who've never seen a real pony."

"I should think you'd have wanted to horsewhip the men," Grandma said to Grandpa.

"Oh, he did, Grandma, but when they told how much Misty meant to poor little city children, well, what could he do?" asked Maureen.

Paul sat up very straight, thinking out his words carefully. "We want to give the money to Uncle Clarence Lee," he said, "and when he gets to be a great big preacher, maybe he'll want to send Maureen and me away to school."

"And if he does," came Maureen's high voice, "I'll study to be a horse doctor."

Grandpa seemed to have a choking spell. He pulled out his red bandanna handkerchief; it almost matched his face.

"Consarn it all," he spluttered and gulped, "I must of got one of them kinks-bush catkins in my gullet."

"Clarence, did you *let* the children sell Misty?"

Grandpa Beebe took a long time folding his handkerchief and getting it back into his pocket. Then he looked sideways, from Paul to Maureen and back again. He cleared his throat. At last he said, "What else could I do, Ida? Misty is theirn. Besides, them men was dead right!"

The silence around the little table seemed never-ending. It was Grandma Beebe who broke it, speaking very softly. "Now I know what you meant, Clarence, when you said the children done a heap of growing up. They had a mill day, too."

Again the silence held them together while each one braved his own thoughts. Suddenly, a sharp siren pierced the quiet. It went through the house like a streak of lightning.

Grandma clutched the table in alarm.

"Don't be so twitchy, Ida. You know that was just the fire whistle calling volunteers to ready up the Pony Penning Grounds."

"Oh, I plumb forgot about all the big doin's."

"Grandma," asked Maureen, "could I go with Paul to help the firemen?"

48

Grandma laughed, but there was a catch in her voice. "To-night I guess I'd let you move the sands of the White Hill if you had a mind to. Go along. All of you. I got a mighty big letter to write to Richmond."

Chapter 4

THE PICTURE-TAKERS' PLANS

OUT THE kitchen door, down the steps, through the barnyard, Paul and Maureen ran.

Geese and turkeys, guinea hens and chicks, flew out of their way. Pigs ran snorting and squealing into the pens. But the ponies came running toward them, jostling each other to be first. Some pinned their ears back, driving the others away. To them Paul and Maureen meant good things. Corn. Water. A good hard gallop.

Misty bustled in among the other ponies, scaring them away with her threatening teeth. She wanted to get closest to Paul and Maureen.

"You're the littlest one," Paul whispered, "but you act the biggest." He laced his fingers into her mane and led her into her own stall. For a second his face tightened. "Maybe," he told her, "when you come back from New York, you'll be old enough for me to ride."

He dropped a handful of corn into her feed box and while she was busy nibbling it, he quickly closed the door behind her.

Maureen had already bridled Watch Eyes, the pony with the white eyes. She held another bridle out for Paul.

"We got to find Mr. Van Meter and Mr. Jacobs before they meet Grandma," she said.

Paul took the bridle. He sorted the ponies with his eyes and selected Trinket, a lively mare, taller than the others. He slipped the reins over her head and the bit into her mouth. He fastened the cheek strap. Then he vaulted up, ready to go.

Grandpa, pitchfork in hand, came to see them off.

"Ye done a big thing," he said, his eyes warm with admiration. "We can't keep nobody to the end-time, anyhow. They got to grow up. And usually they got to go away." He shoved his pitchfork in the soil and cleaned off the tines slowly to help his thinking. "Now the way for us all to take the sting off our thoughts is to keep busy as hummer-birds. We got to get so plumb tired we can't lay awake by night. We'll jes' turn in, turn over, turn out. That's what I'm going to do!"

Fastening the gate, he brandished his pitchfork over his head and was off, singing in a husky voice,

"Oh, they're wild and woolly and full of fleas,
And never been curried below the knees. . . ."

Down the lane, along the hard-packed trail to the Pony Penning Grounds, Paul and Maureen rode. The sun was slipping into the pocket of the horizon. Dusk was gathering, but Watch Eyes and Trinket knew their way. Often they had been entered in the races during Pony Penning Week. When they reached the grounds, they turned in of their own accord.

"You're early for the races," a man in a fisherman's cap laughed up at Paul and Maureen. "By the way, did two men find you? I understand they're picture-takers, come all the way from New York."

"They here now?" asked Paul.

The fisherman pointed his finger toward the pony pens. "They're down yonder in the big pen, conferencing with the fire chief."

52

Paul and Maureen could see them now. Mr. Jacobs sitting on the fence, writing in a notebook, Mr. Van Meter nodding to the fire chief while his eyes wandered over the empty pens and out across the water to the masts of the oyster boats.

Paul and Maureen rode up to them. The faces of the men turned quickly.

"Hello, you two," Mr. Van Meter called.

The fire chief mopped the sweat beaded on his forehead. "I'm mighty relieved you've come," he said. "Wilbur Wimbrow just asked me for a wiry somebody to do a special job for him. That's you, Paul. And the ladies of the Auxiliary need you to help wash dishes in the dining hall, Maureen."

"We did come to help, Chief," Paul answered, fixing his eyes on the ground, "but mostly we came to tell the movie men we changed our minds—about Misty."

Mr. Jacobs hastily stuffed his papers into his pocket and looked up with a startled expression.

Mr. Van Meter ran a fingernail across the rail of the fence to scratch out his thoughts.

"You—you haven't changed your minds?" asked Maureen in sudden alarm.

"I don't know," said Mr. Van Meter. "Your grandpa, how does he feel about it?"

"Why," gulped Paul, "he told Grandma at supper tonight that you were dead right."

Both children nodded, not daring to trust their voices.

Mr. Van Meter put out his hand. He reached up and took Maureen's first, then Paul's. "It's a deal, then," he said in a very quiet voice, "and I think you know we'll take the best possible care of Misty. We'll fly her to New York the day after Pony Penning."

Paul and Maureen counted the days in their minds. They had less than a week.

After a little while Paul said to the fire chief, "We'll tie Watch Eyes and Trinket. Then we want to go to work."

54

The fire chief saw the look in their eyes. "Wilbur Wimbrow is over near the track, Paul," he said with understanding. "He's having trouble installing the loud-speaker. And the ladies are cleaning the cupboards, Maureen. Seem's like you two must have sensed how shorthanded we were tonight."

All that week, day after day, Paul and Maureen spent at the Pony Penning Grounds, helping Chincoteague get ready for its big celebration. Paul liked working alongside the volunteer firemen. They were broad-shouldered and strong; yet they treated him as if he were one of them. When they needed someone to squeeze into a small spot, they never said, "We could use a youngster here." Always it was, "Paul, he can do it for you. He's wiry as any billy goat."

Once or twice Paul caught himself whistling as he worked. Then suddenly in the midst of a tune he would remember, and fall silent.

Maureen worked in the hall where the huge Pony Penning dinner was to be served. All the dishes had to be washed, and fresh white paper tacked on the long tables. Cutting and tack-ing the paper was fun, but washing the stacks upon stacks of dishes unused since last Pony Penning seemed a waste of time to her. "Why don't we just dust them off?" she suggested in a small voice.

When everyone laughed, she slipped away to Pony Ranch to help Grandpa. She found Mr. Jacobs there, sitting in the doorway of the corn house, taking notes on the backs of old envelopes.

"Could I ask something?" she said shyly.

Mr. Jacobs looked up and gave a friendly nod. "I'd like that. Ask all the questions you want."

It was always hardest to begin. Maureen twisted one leg about the other uncomfortably. "Is New York," she blurted out at last, "is New York a place where the sea winds blow?"

Mr. Jacobs answered quietly and earnestly. "Yes," he said, "but not as softly as here."

"And could a pony—I mean, could a body smell the sea?"

Mr. Jacobs' eyes grew deep and thoughtful. "Yes, sometimes. But you've got to sift it through city smells. It's far away, like something in a dream."

Misty butted right into their conversation. Grandma's white curtains were on the line, and Misty had swooped under them. Now she came waltzing along, trailing the curtains far out behind her like a wedding veil.

This sent Maureen and Mr. Jacobs off into peals of laughter, and brought Grandma out on a run. She caught up her curtains to wash them all over again without so much as a cross word for Misty.

The days flew by, but the nighttimes did not go quickly at all.

"Did you hear a lot of owls whooing last night?" Maureen asked Paul on the morning before the roundup.

"'Course I did. Anyone would hear screechy critters like that. But what was even louder was the apples making a thud when they fell."

"Do you . . . do you hear them, too, Paul?"

Paul nodded. "I counted eight. And twigs a-snapping like rifle shots, and the ponies tearing the grass as noisy as Grandma ripping old bed sheets to make dust rags out of them."

In the midst of their talk, Mr. Van Meter came driving up in an old rented car. He got out and sat down on the kitchen stoop so that he was looking up at them.

"We plan to take the roundup scene tomorrow," he said. "We're anxious to get good shots of the roundup men driving the wild ponies to Tom's Cove over on Assateague Island. You've been on the roundup, Paul. You'll know where we should set our cameras. Will you help?"

Paul lifted his chin and stood up very straight. "I'll help," he said.

"Mr. Jacobs will go with you," Mr. Van Meter went on. "But I'll be waiting here on Chincoteague to get pictures of the ponies swimming across the channel. Maureen, will you help me? You could tell me just where the ponies will land."

"I have to be here," Maureen answered. "After the wild ponies are swimmed across, I always help drive them into the pony pens."

58

"Good! Then everything's settled. Paul will meet Mr. Jacobs at Old Dominion Point at seven-thirty sharp, and I will meet you there a little later, Maureen."

The boy and the girl nodded politely.

"It'll be just as exciting as going on the roundup," Paul said, but his words were braver than his voice.

"It's funny," Maureen confided to Paul after Mr. Van Meter had driven away, "instead of hating Mr. Van Meter and Mr. Jacobs, I like them. I like them both."

"I do, too," admitted Paul. "And sometimes when I hear Grandma brag on 'Clarence Lee at college' I feel good inside."

"Like the time you turned the wild Phantom loose and let her go back to Assateague?"

"Yes, like that," Paul said.

Chapter 5

CAUGHT IN THE PONY-WAY

ON THE dawn of the roundup day, Paul tiptoed to his window. He crouched on the floor, his arms resting on the sill. A full yellow moon, flat as a tiddlywink, hung low in the western sky. A grayness was rising in the east and the sea, too, was a ball of gray cotton. It was the hour the roundup men would be leaving Chincoteague, loading their mounts onto the scow that would ferry them over to the island of the wild things.

In his mind Paul could hear the sound of the motor and the waves slapping against the heavy timbers of the scow. He could hear the blowing and snorting of the horses, the clipped, nervous speech of the men. Once he had been one of them. Single-handed, he had captured the wild Phantom and her baby, Misty. How long ago that seemed! He wondered if the Phantom would be caught this year. His body broke out in sweat just thinking about her. How beautiful she was! How hard he and Maureen had worked to tame the wildness out of her! But in the end they had given her back her freedom.

"Some critters is made to be wild," a voice said behind him.

Paul scrambled to his feet, startled.

It was Grandpa Beebe in his nightshirt. "I couldn't sleep for thinkin' about Misty's mamma," he said. "So I tipped to yer room. Figured ye might be awake."

"Grandpa!"

"Yes, boy."

Paul's words came in a rush. "Grandpa! If you hopped Watch Eyes and galloped to the mooring place, you could stop the scow. You could join the roundup. You could," Paul whispered tensely, "you could make sure the Phantom escaped."

The little bedroom was very still. Paul could not see Grandpa's face, but he could hear his troubled sigh.

"'Tain't like ye, Paul," Grandpa said at last. "'Twould be downright dishonest. Besides, when the roundup men comes upon the Phantom, they'll be puny as dustin' straws in a blow. Ye can almost count on her escapin' this year. She's been caught oncet. She ain't goin' to let it happen again. Now slip on your pants," he said. "Ye can help me do the chores afore ye have to meet the movie men."

Sharp at seven-thirty Paul was waiting at Old Dominion Point. A few early visitors from the mainland were tramping about expectantly, asking questions of each other.

"How did the wild ponies get to Assateague in the first place?"

"When was the first Pony Penning held?"

"I heard it's the oldest roundup in the United States and the biggest wild west show of the east!" said a man with a kodak in his hands and three children at his heels. "It's different, too. They swim the wild ponies across to Chincoteague."

Paul walked away. He could not bring himself to talk about the roundup and Pony Penning. "It's sacred, kind of," he said to himself. "And it takes somebody like Grandpa or Miss Vic to make folks understand about it." He was glad when he heard the chugging of a motor and caught sight of Joe Selby's oyster boat with Mr. Jacobs and a stranger aboard. He rolled his pants above his knees and waded out into the water.

"Halloo-oo-oo," he shouted, waving his arms. "I'm here!"

The boat nosed over and he clambered aboard. Mr. Jacobs was barefoot, too, and he was ripping open cartons of films.

"Paul," he said, "this is Mr. Winter, one of our cameramen, who came down to Chincoteague last night."

Paul looked up at the lean, serious young man. His shy

"how do" was lost in the sputter of the engine as the boat turned and headed out into the channel.

"And you know Joe here," Mr. Jacobs nodded toward the man at the tiller.

Paul smiled at the weather-creased face of Joe Selby. Many a time he had gone oystering in this very boat.

"I hear Grandpa Beebe is a pretty good weather prophet. What did he say, Paul? Clear skies?" asked Mr. Jacobs, squinting anxiously at the clouds.

Paul blushed. "I didn't ask him." How could he explain that he and Grandpa had been more concerned with Misty's mother?

"Well, Joe here thinks it won't rain. Never has rained on Pony Penning Day. Never will, he says."

The talk stopped.

The wind dried Paul's wet legs. He shivered a little from cold and excitement. He watched the people on Chincoteague blur into a cloud, then watched the cloud slowly wisp out until it stretched far up the beach.

Ahead of him lay the waving grasses of Assateague, and on and beyond the pine woods and the sea. If he half-closed his eyes, the tops of the pines became the mane of a horse and the White Hill the cap of a rider, and the whole island was riding in advance of their boat, looking after her like any outrider, protecting her from the mighty waves of the Atlantic.

Suddenly the motor went quiet, cutting off his thoughts.

"We're in the shallows now," Joe called out. "Close as we can get to Tom's Cove."

Camera on shoulders, film held high above the water, the two movie men jumped overboard.

Paul followed. The soft bottom squinched up between his toes. How different this was from going on the roundup! Instead of pounding over the marshland, shouting and driving the wild ponies, here he was, splashing ashore, as peaceful as on a Sunday school picnic.

But Mr. Jacobs was not calm and quiet, and his eyes were no longer dark and cool. They threw sparks like horseshoes on a pavement.

"Paul," he said sharply, "from which direction will the ponies come? We want to set our cameras close enough to catch the wild look in their eyes."

Paul thought carefully before replying. "The roundup men drive 'em down to that little grazing ground yonder. But they come from"—he wheeled around and pointed a finger to the deep woods that formed the backbone of the island—"they come from . . ."

Paul's sentence hung in mid air. A rolling boom of noise! Dust clouds swirling! And hulking out of the woods some dark misshapen thing! It might have been a prehistoric monster or a giant kicking up clods of earth for all the form it had. But whatever it was, it hugged along the ground like puffs of smoke on a windless day. Now the shape fell apart! It was the men on horseback driving the wild herds to Tom's Cove. They were coming earlier than anyone had expected. Much earlier.

Paul and the two men were blocking the pony-way! The

ponies would be coming right at them. How could he get the men and the camera to safety?

A daring thought crossed his mind. Let them stay in the pony-way! Let them stay! Let the wild things come dead-heat at the camera. "They got horse sense," he thought. "They'll split around us."

He skinned off his white shirt and buried it in the sand. The ponies must not shy away from a billowing white object.

"Follow me!" he shouted, running directly toward the noisy, swirling mass.

The cameraman was young. He could run almost as fast as Paul, even with a clumsy camera to carry. Along the hard-packed sand, across the meadow marsh, up a little rise the three of them ran.

"Here!" shouted Paul, pointing to the camera.

It was too late to explain his plan. The dark racing monster was no longer a nebulous thing. Wild ponies and men on mounts were taking shape, coming around the horseshoe curve of Tom's Cove, splitting the air with yells and whinnies and pounding hooves, like thunder rolling nearer and nearer.

Mr. Jacobs was standing close to the cameraman, his eyes darting nervously from the oncoming ponies to the overcast sky. He nodded to Paul that he understood. If the plan worked, the ponies would break up in two bunches around the camera. He would get a closeup of the wildest scene of the roundup.

And suddenly the sun struck through the clouds like a powerful searchlight. Manes, tails, sweating bodies were high-lighted with red and gold.

"Now! Now!" Paul heard himself yelling. "This is it!" Why was that cameraman so slow? What was he waiting for? Was there ever a sight so wild? It was wilder than thunder and lightning. Wilder than wind.

He clenched his hands behind him to keep from knocking the camera over. This man Winter was as cold as his name. Paul hated him. He had given up going on the roundup for

him, for a man who stood frozen. A man who waited, waited, waited, when all around him the wild things were blowing and screaming.

And just when he could stand the delay no longer came the clicking, clicking sound of the camera close in his ear. Mr. Winter was grinding now. And just in time. The ponies were plunging at him, their eyes white ringed, their nostrils dilated until the red lining showed like blood. Now they were splitting in two bunches, swerving around the camera, coming so close that their tails whisked it.

Paul drew a long breath of relief as he turned to look at Mr. Jacobs.

"He knows just when," laughed Mr. Jacobs weakly.

Chapter 6

HORSE-DOCTOR PAUL

THE PONIES began to slacken their pace. They were coming to the sweetest grass on Assateague. The roundup men, almost as blown as the horses, drew rein.

Suddenly Paul forgot the cameramen; he was a horseman now. "Look!" A choked cry escaped him. "A mare's hurt, terrible hurt. Look at her limp. Her colt can outrun her."

He raced across the wiry grass to the men resting their mounts. "What's the matter of her, Mr. Wimbrow?" he called anxiously.

Mr. Wimbrow took off his fisherman's cap and wiped the perspiration from his forehead. "Heel string's cut," he said tiredly. "Likely she cut it on an oyster shell."

68

The mare tucked her forelegs beneath her and lay down to rest, as if she knew the roundup was only half over. She was a pinto with splashy black and white markings. She might have been beautiful, but now she was just a crippled captive. A captive who seemed content to rest while her puzzled colt and stallion watched over her.

"You going to swim her across the channel?" Paul asked.

"Reckon we will," Mr. Wimbrow said. "The salt water will clean the cut better'n any man-made medicine."

Paul nodded. If Wilbur Wimbrow thought swimming wouldn't hurt the mare, it wouldn't. He turned to study the milling mob of ponies, watching the stallions gather in their own families. Every now and then a mare would break away, and the stallion would herd her back into his band with galloping hooves and bared teeth. At last they were all neatly grouped like classes in school.

"I hanker to see the Phantom," Paul thought aloud, "but I hope I don't!" He wondered at himself. One time he had so wanted to capture her. Now he so wanted her to remain free. He could not bring himself to ask the men if she had been caught. From one bunch of ponies to another he went. There were blacks and chestnuts and bays and pintos, but nowhere among them was Misty's beautiful wild mother with the white map on her withers.

"She didn't get caught!" he whispered with a fierce gladness. He wanted to throw back his head and whinny his relief to the whole wide world.

Instead, he belly-flopped in the grass, laughing softly to himself. The sun poured down on his back, warmed him through. All around, the wild creatures were grazing, their legs scissor blades, opening and closing, opening and closing, as they moved from one delicious clump of grass to another. Paul felt strangely comforted. Out here on Assateague, with the wild things so near, he could push aside unhappy thoughts. Maybe Friday would never come. He pulled a blade of grass and slid it between his teeth, savoring the salty taste. For a long time he lay quite still, lulled by the wind and the waves and the pleasant sound of the ponies cropping the grasses. It was not until

he heard boats starting up their motors that he went back to
the cameramen.

"The tide's ebbing bare," he told them. "The men'll be driving the ponies into the water soon. They're going to need all the

boats to make a kind of causeway for the ponies to swim from Assateague to Chincoteague."

He dug up his shirt, shook it free of sand, and pulled it over his head. Then he waded out to Joe Selby's boat.

Everything was working according to plan. The boats, spitting and sputtering, were lining up to form a sea lane across the channel. On the beach the roundup men were closing in, drawing a tight circle around the ponies. A sudden explosion of lusty yells, and now the animals were plunging into the sea! Men's cries mingled with the screaming of ponies and the wild clatter of birds overhead. The channel was boiling with noise.

Paul's eyes and ears sharpened. He felt he belonged neither to the roundup men nor to the cameramen. He was an excited onlooker, like the visitors from Norfolk, from Washington, from Philadelphia. He watched the hurt mare and her colt stumble into the foam. The water seemed to revive the mare.

"Look at her colt!" he laughed aloud. "He's getting a free ride!"

Sure enough, the colt's muzzle was anchored firmly on his mother's back. It seemed to comfort the mare, to give her new strength.

Four or five tow-headed boys were swimming alongside the ponies. They wanted to be ready in case a foal needed life-saving. They remembered how Paul had rescued the drowning baby Misty. But this year the colts were expert as swimmers in a water carnival, and not one needed help.

The first ponies were scrambling up the beach at Chinco-

72

teague now, their coats curried by the water and the noonday
sun. The blacks were no longer shaggy and dusty but took on
the shininess of satin, and the chestnuts glistened like burnished
copper.

"Slick as moles!" Paul laughed to himself.

He wanted to get to them quickly, eager as any sightseer. "Let's put in to shore," he yelled to Joe Selby.

The scow with the roundup men was landing alongside them. Wilbur Wimbrow's arm went up, signaling for Paul to come.

The boy welcomed an excuse to be with the horsemen. "They need me," he said to Mr. Jacobs as he leaped over the side of the boat.

"That hurt mare's got to have some first aid," Mr. Wimbrow told Paul. "Your fingers are fine as a mother-woman's. Us men'll hold her quiet while you lay these cigarettes in her cut. The tobacco'll burn it clean."

He handed two cigarettes to Paul and took the bandanna handkerchief from around his neck. "You can use this for a bandage," he said. "It'll stay the blood."

Grandpa Beebe, gathering his rope, stepped up behind Mr. Wimbrow. "Leave me rope the hurt mare fer ye," he said.

Mr. Wimbrow was glad of fresh hands to help. "After we doctor her," he told Grandpa, "I'd like it if Paul and Maureen'd lead her over to my place. If she's driven to the pony pens along with the mob, she's liable to get tromped on."

"Better off by herself," Grandpa agreed. "What you want done with her colt?"

"We'll drive him to the Pony Penning Grounds with the others. He's big enough to be sold with the other colts."

Grandpa Beebe easily roped the mare. Then he talked to her in the voice he saved for wild things. "Easy there. Easy, girl. Ye're not hurted bad."

74

The crowds closed in to watch.

"Why don't they shoot her?" asked a well-meaning visitor wearing Oxford glasses.

"Why!" barked Grandpa. "For the same reason yer family didn't aim a gun at ye when ye lost yer nacheral sight."

The people cheered for Grandpa and pressed in closer.

"Go ahead," Mr. Wimbrow nodded to Paul. "We got her."

Paul tore the paper from the cigarettes. He picked up the hurt leg, bending it at the knee. Gently but firmly he laid the tobacco in the cut. It was good to be helping, not just watching. Now he knew how good Grandma must feel when she took care of a sick neighbor. Maybe he and Maureen would both be horse doctors when they grew up. Maybe they would live in the old lighthouse on Assateague. Then they could see whenever a wild creature was hurt. All these thoughts spun around in his mind as he tied the bandanna securely.

"Paul, you leg up on Trinket now," Mr. Wimbrow said. He beckoned to Maureen, who was mounted on Watch Eyes and holding Trinket for Paul. "Then you two lead the mare down behind Old Dominion Lodge so's she can't see her colt go off without her."

Grandpa and Mr. Wimbrow tied a connecting rein between the hurt mare and Trinket and Watch Eyes. Then they faced her out to sea while the roundup men roped her colt and headed for the Pony Penning Grounds. A little moment and it was over. The trembling of the mare quieted. Her neighing became no more than a whimper. She limped numbly along between Watch Eyes and Trinket.

"Paul," said Maureen as they headed for Mr. Wimbrow's house, "seems this mare's got enough trouble without having her colt taken away from her too."

Paul was busy trying to hold Trinket to the slow pace of the mare.

"'Course she's got enough trouble," he said at last, "but up to Mr. Wimbrow's house she won't be able to hear the colt whinkerin' for her all night long." He rode on in silence for a moment. Then he added, "Maybe it's like a twitch."

"What's like a twitch?"

"Humpf," snorted Paul. "You wanting to be a horse doctor and don't even know what a twitch is."

"I do too know what a twitch is. It's nothing but a piece of rope twisted around a horse's nose to make him forget where his pain's at."

"Well," said Paul, "this mare's foot probably hurts so bad she can't fret about losing her colt."

Maureen nodded her head.

Chapter 7

THE BEST KIND OF WINKERS

GRANDPA WAS already at home when Paul and Maureen arrived. He was trying to seem very happy.

"Childern," he shouted, "look-a-here. Ever see such a whopping big watermelon? And it's frosty cold, asides." He held it high to show that it was beaded with icy sweat. "Grandma says if we're going to eat it in our hands we got to stay outside." He winked happily.

Grandma Beebe came out of the house with a pan of steaming water, a bar of brown soap, and washcloths. She set the pan on a bench in the shade. "Now," she said brightly, "wash up good, and let the wind dry you off. I been making a plummy cake for the Ladies' Auxiliary and my kitchen's hot as a griddle. Out here it's nice and cool." She looked up at Paul and Maureen. "What's the matter of you two? You glued to Watch Eyes and Trinket?" But she smiled as she said it.

Paul and Maureen slid to their feet and led their mounts to the big shed.

"Don't let your ponies stomp on my biddies," Grandma called after them.

There was a chorus of neighing as the horses that had been left behind greeted the ones that had been away. Misty's neigh was a high squeal of happiness. Paul and Maureen stopped to rough up her mane and stroke her nose. Then they hung up their bridles and joined Grandpa at the wash bench, while Misty tagged along.

"There's a letter come from Clarence Lee this morning," Grandma was saying as she laid a red-checked cloth on the picnic table. "He's in the college all right, studying to be a minister."

"A minister, eh?" Grandpa Beebe straightened up and planted his feet wide apart. "I'm a-danged," he laughed softly. "To think I sired a minister! Why, I'm that proud I'm liable to go around with my chest stickin' out like a pewter pigeon."

"You mean pouter pigeon, Clarence."

"Well, let's not gibble-gabble. We got us a lot of watermelon to eat. And I've brung some new little carrots for Misty."

Grandma had made crab cakes and baked them in clam shells, and she had black-eyed peas and corn pone with wild honey. And Grandpa was all excited about the deep pink of his watermelon and the blackness of the seeds. "'Taint only something noble to look at," he exclaimed, "but whoever tasted a melon so downright juicy and sweet?"

Pony Ranch seemed to draw close about Paul and Maureen. They could not help feeling comforted by Grandpa's and Grandma's happiness.

Maybe, if no one thought about Friday, it would never come. Maybe they could go on picnicking forever, with Misty coming to them and offering to shake hands until all the carrots were gone, and the chickens fighting over the watermelon rinds and rushing for each seed that was dropped.

"I declare!" Grandma said, her eyes fixed on the whirling chickens. "It took me to be a grownup afore I figgered out why they call that shoal up north of here 'Hens and Chickens.' It's

80

plain as the nose on your face that they do it 'cause the water swirls and closes in like hens and chicks after a morsel to eat!"

Grandpa clucked his tongue in admiration. "Ida! I never knowed the reason either!"

When the picnic was over, Paul got up and stretched himself. He squinted at the sky between the pines and found the position of the sun. "They're just about fixing to call the bronc-busting contest over at the Pony Penning Grounds," he said to Grandpa. "Reckon I'll ride."

Grandma caught her breath. "Don't let him do it, Clarence," she cried in alarm. "He'll be killed outright."

"There, there, Ida." Grandpa's voice was the same one he had used on the hurt mare. "He'll not get killed. Leastaways, not outright," he grinned. "Y'see, Ida, Paul and Maureen is like nervous hosses. They got to wear winkers to keep from seein' things comin' up from behind. My grandpap used to say" —and here Grandpa Beebe began rubbing the stubble in his ears as if he were enormously pleased with his memory—"he used to say, 'Clarence, keepin' busy is the best kind of winkers. If ye keep busy today, ye can't see tomorrow comin' up.' That's what he said."

Underneath his eyebrows Grandpa's eyes had a merry gleam. "Go 'long, Paul. Pick out a tough pony and ride 'im till he's dauncy. I'd sure give my last two teeth to trade places with ye."

Chapter 8

A WILD ONE FOR WILD-PONY PAUL

WHEN PAUL and Maureen rode into the Pony Penning Grounds, the loud-speaker was blasting at full strength. "Ladies and gentlemen, Jack Winter of New York City is making his way over to the chute."

"That's the cameraman!" Paul told Maureen excitedly. "He's going to ride in the contest!"

They tied their mounts quickly, running to the corral just in time to see the young New Yorker come bolting out of the chute on a white spook of a horse. His hands were clutched in the horse's mane, and he was gripping hard with his knees. But his feet were not locked around the pony's barrel. He looked like a rider in the bareback class at a horse show.

Paul was screaming at him, "Lock your feet around his belly. Lock your feet around . . ."

But his words thinned into nothing. The white spook had planted his forefeet in the earth and was lashing the sky with his heels. One second . . . two seconds . . . three seconds . . . four, five, six, barely seven seconds, and Mr. Winter was plummeting through space, then falling to earth with a thud.

A bugle of triumph tore the stillness that followed. Then the freed animal went snaking around the corral until a round-up man roped him.

Shakily Mr. Winter got to his feet, stumbled out the gate held open for him, and lost himself in the crowd.

"Give a big hand to Mr. Winter, folks. That's all he'll get," called the voice over the loud-speaker.

The crowd responded with spirited applause.

"Who'll be next, folks? The ten dollars still stands. Who's next?"

Paul's arm shot into the air, but no one saw it.

The voice kept prodding. "How about Delbert Daisy?"

People all around Paul and Maureen were making remarks. "Delbert tried it last year," someone said. "He's too smart to try again."

"I'm a cowboy from Texas," a man with a ten gallon hat drawled, "but I be dogged if I'm ready to pick me a homestead. I'm a reg'lar bronc rider, used to a halter and a belly rope for anchor."

Another stranger agreed. "No siree! No thousand pounds of wild horseflesh under me without something to hold on to. Not me!"

"Who's next, folks? Who's next?" the voice hammered.

The crowds around the corral were banked solid. Paul could not wedge between them to climb the fence. He and Maureen finally wriggled underneath it.

Inside the corral Paul's hand went up again.

This time everyone saw.

"Look, everybody! Paul Beebe's next," the voice bawled out. "Ten dollars to Paul if he can stay aboard for thirty seconds. Stand back, Maureen. That's his sister, folks. Stand flat against the fence, Maureen."

Maureen clutched at her throat. They were going to let her stay in the corral! She stood back as far as she could, leaning hard against the rails, with the people pressing against her on the other side.

"Let out a wild one for Wild-Pony Paul!" came the voice.

Paul was gone. He was climbing the fence of the chute, swinging his leg over an unbroken pony, gripping the strands of tangled mane as if they were reins.

"Who's he riding?" someone cried.

There was a pause.

Then the announcer's voice cracked with excitement. "A wild one it is! Red Demon—a she-devil on hooves. Those aren't her ears, folks, they're horns!"

A hush of expectation fell over the onlookers.

"Be you ready, Paul?"

A thin voice answered, "Turn 'er loose."

Every eye was riveted on the closed gate of the chute. Now it burst open and Red Demon, a chestnut with a blaze, shot out bucking and twisting. In a quick flash of seeing, her white-ringed eyes swept the corral. Suddenly she spied a tree at the far end. She hurtled toward it, not straight like a bullet, but in a tortuous, weaving line, calculating, deadly.

Paul tried to capture the rhythm of her muscles. He leaned back, gripping with his thighs, pushing inward and backward with his knees, turning and twisting with her, writhing like a corkscrew.

The crowds watched, horrified. This was the thrill they had come to see.

Maureen hid her face in her hands, listening. She heard the earthquake of hooves as the Red Demon headed for the tree, heard a man's voice rasp out, "He's going to get hung up in that pine!" She waited for the crash, but there was none. Stealthily she peered between her fingers. They were not going to crack up! The wild pony was swerving around the tree and Paul was making the spine-wrenching turn with her. He was still on!

Now the weight of Paul enraged Red Demon. Birds and flies could be removed with a swish of the tail. But no mere swishing would remove this clinging creature. There had to be violence. She brought her head and shoulder to the ground, then jerked up with a sudden sharpness. The boy's head jounced down and shot up in unison.

A woman shrieked.

Maureen grabbed the back of her own neck. She felt as if it had been snapped in two.

"Hang on!" she screamed. "Hang on!"

Red and glaring, the hot sun struck down on the two wild things. It seemed to weld them together like bronze figures heated in the same furnace. They were all of one piece. The boy's arms were rigid bands of bronze, and his hair did not fly and toss with the rocketing of the pony—it hung down, sweat-matted between his eyes, like the forelock of a stallion. It was hard to tell which was wilder, boy or pony.

"Fourteen seconds . . . fifteen seconds," the voice over the loud-speaker blared.

And still the two figures were one, the boy's arms unbending, his legs soldered in place.

That lone tree at the end of the corral! It seemed to bewitch Red Demon. Again she rushed at it, head lowered as if to gore it with her devil ears. A thousand throats gasped as she whiplashed around it again, and then once again, each time missing by a wink.

And still Paul held on.

"Twenty seconds . . . twenty-one seconds . . ."

The power of the sun seemed to strengthen as the seconds wore on. Now it fused the two wild creatures, making molten metal of them. In fluid motion, horse and boy were riding out the fire together. Together, they dipped and rose and spurted through space, now part of the earth, now part of the sky.

Maureen felt her knees giving way. "Please! Please! Someone stop them! Oh, stop them!" She tried to brace herself

against the fence to keep from falling. The beat of Red Demon's hooves continued to pound hard and steady in her ears. She closed her eyes for a second, then opened them.

Something was happening! The molten mass was bursting in two. Everything went black before her eyes. When next she opened them, Paul was lying beside her. Then they were both picking themselves up, laughing feebly. Paul was no longer the bronzed rider on a bronzed horse. He was a dirt-streaked, pale-faced boy in faded jeans.

All about them half-frenzied visitors were swarming over the fence rails, men and women laughing and crying both, asking questions and answering themselves. And over and above the noise, the voice on the loud-speaker never stopped. "Thirty-three seconds! Thirty-three seconds! Paul rode her dizzy. The ten dollars goes to Paul Beebe."

Chapter 9

OFF IN A SWIRL OF MIST

PAUL SPOKE in breathless jerks as they edged away from the crowd. "I'm going to give the ten dollars—to Mr. Van Meter—to see that Misty has some carrots each day," he told Maureen.

But Mr. Van Meter refused the money. "We'll see that Misty gets her carrots, Paul. You save your money for something very special," he said with a wise look.

"What would that be?"

"I don't know, but something special always turns up when my youngsters have ten dollars saved. Now you two better go home. You've had a hard day."

The sun was throwing long shadows by the time Paul and Maureen arrived back at Pony Ranch. There was not much talk during supper that night, and afterward the boy and girl were too tired to enter Watch Eyes or Trinket in the night races to be held at the Pony Penning Grounds.

Paul helped Grandpa water the ponies while Maureen sat on a chicken coop drawing pictures of Misty. She worked with

quick strokes because Misty seldom remained still. While the pony was drinking at the water barrel, Maureen drew a side view of her, the side with the map of the United States on it. And while she tagged after Paul, Maureen sketched a funny little back view—the softly rounded white rump and the long tail that swished from side to side when she walked. Maureen laughed aloud as she tried to put the swishes on paper.

Paul and Grandpa came to look over her shoulder.

"By smoke! I'm a jumpin' mullet if there ain't a strong favorance to Misty!" Grandpa said.

"It's not bad," Paul agreed.

"Don't she look like a little girl wearing her grandma's long dress?" Maureen giggled. Then her face sobered.

Paul was staring at the pictures, at all of them. "You can make me some—if you like," he said in a low voice.

Misty went back to the water barrel for another long, cooling drink, then stood quite still watching Maureen sketch and erase and erase and sketch. The evening breeze was stirring. Soon Misty would settle down to the business of grazing by moonlight. But right now, when it was neither night nor day, she was content to snuff the winds and to look about her.

She came over to Maureen and breathed very softly down her neck. She nudged the bread board on which the drawing paper was tacked. Then, as if she were posing, she turned her head slightly, looking out over the marshland, waiting for night to close in.

Maureen sketched on. The pricked ears, the blaze on her face, the soft pink underlip with its few lady whiskers, the mane lifted by the small wind.

At last she had four pictures for Paul and four for herself. She started to say good-night to Misty, but Grandma was watching from the doorway.

"Let's see what you've done, Maureen," she called out. "As a girl I was always one for drawing, too."

Maureen showed Grandma the pictures and smiled at her

praise. Then she put the ones for Paul on a shelf in his room and went to her own room. There she laid her page of sketches on her pillow, and fell into a deep, exhausted slumber.

Toward morning, sounds pecked at her sleep. She dreamed she was riding Red Demon on an oyster-shell road, and the tattoo of hooves pinged sharper and sharper in her ears.

She awoke to the sound of hammer strokes. With sudden anxiety she was out of bed, dressing, hurrying to join Paul and Grandpa. The hammer strokes could mean but one thing. They were building a crate for Misty. She must get to them quickly —to see they built it big enough, strong enough.

"If I don't have to eat any breakfast," she pleaded with Grandma, "I'll make up for it tomorrow. Honest I will."

To Maureen's astonishment Grandma agreed. "No griddle cakes this morning," she said. "They'd stick in your throat and lump in your stummick. Only this tiny glass of milk."

Instead of an everyday glass tumbler, Grandma was pouring the milk in the ruby-colored glass, the one her own grandmother had left her. Maureen somehow managed to drink all of it.

When she burst out of the house, the floor of the crate was already built.

"Maureen!" Grandpa called to her. "You hurry down marsh and gather driftwood. Paul, you look in that bunch of scantlings. See if there's anything we can use. I'm a-danged if lumber around Pony Ranch ain't scarce as two-headed cats."

The finished crate was an odd-looking object. Uprights had been splintered from an old gate, laths taken from a deserted chicken roost, and driftwood from who knows where; but so much care and measuring had gone into the making of it that to Paul and Maureen and Grandpa it did not look rough-made at all.

"Snug, ain't it?" said Grandpa, forcing a smile. "And Paul's gathered a big enough bundle of salt grass to last her the hull day."

"'Member when we readied the stall for Phantom?" asked Maureen very softly. "Readying a crate is not . . . is not . . ."

Grandpa snapped his fingers. "Consarn it all!" he sputtered. "I plumb forgot the pine shatters. Paul and Maureen, you gather some nice smelly pine shatters from off'n the floor of the woods. Nothin' makes a better cushion for pony feet as pine shatters. Besides, it smells to their liking. *Every*thing'll smell to her liking—salt grass, driftwood, pine shatters."

Taking the wheelbarrow and an old broom, Paul and Maureen headed for the woods.

"Grandpa can think of more things for us to do!" Maureen scolded as she swept the pine needles in a heap.

"It's just his way of putting our winkers on, Maureen."

Scarcely were the pine needles dumped onto the floor of the crate than Grandpa pointed to the sky.

"Be that winged critter a gull or a plane?"

The beat of engines was the answer. A silver plane came sweeping down on Pony Ranch, now circling it, now banking, now turning into the wind, landing, taxiing right up to the gate!

Barnyard creatures flew screeching into the air. The older ponies ran snorting for their shed. Only Misty stood her ground. She had seen this strange silver bird before. She had snuffed it carefully from its big nose to its twin tails. There was nothing at all to be afraid of.

Mr. Van Meter and Mr. Jacobs jumped out of the cockpit. They nodded a good-morning to Grandpa, then came right over to Paul and Maureen.

"It makes it easier," Mr. Jacobs hesitated, then tried again. "It makes it easier," he said, "knowing you two *want* to share Misty with boys and girls everywhere. Van and I were saying this morning—if we didn't know we were going to make thousands of children happy, we certainly wouldn't make two sad."

"Maureen!" commanded Paul, and there was something of Grandpa's tone in his voice. "Here's some corn kernels. You

stand by the crate and slip your hand between the boards."

Maureen did as she was told.

"Now hold out the nibbles and call to her."

Maureen's voice faltered, "Come along—little Misty," she sang brokenly, "come—along."

98

Misty hesitated only an instant. Then she stepped onto the friendly pine needles and walked into the crate.

It took Grandpa and Paul, Mr. Van Meter and Mr. Jacobs, and the pilot, too, to load the crate onto the plane.

Maureen stood watching, looking and thinking and trying not to do either.

Suddenly she felt a pair of warm arms folded close about her. She turned and buried her face in Grandma's broad bosom. "Oh, Grandma," she sobbed, "I feel just like a mother who has borned many children. But Misty is my favorite. And it hurts to have her grow up and leave us . . . without even looking back and whinkerin'. She's—" Maureen burst into tears, "she's even eating her grass!"

"She don't understand, honey," comforted Grandma. "She's just a young 'un, all excited in her mind. Children and ponies both get all excited with traveling and their boxed lunches. They seldom cry when they go off. It's the ones left behind does the bellering. Now blow your nose good and don't let Paul see you cry."

After the crate was safely stowed inside the plane, the men came back out and looked from one silent face to another.

"Now we will say good-bye to you all," Mr. Van Meter said quietly. "We will do everything we can to keep Misty well and make her happy. She has a big job in life now. She's got to be a sea horse more than ever, leaving a little trail of happiness in her wake wherever she goes. She's got work to do!"

"Please," asked Maureen, "always each night whisper in Misty's ear that we'll be here a-waiting for her when she's ready to come home."

"Think of it!" said Paul with a crooked smile. "Misty's the first one of the family to see our islands from the air." He turned to Mr. Van Meter. "Do you suppose you could point out the White Hill to her from the air so's she could see where the Spanish galleon was wrecked?"

"I think we could, Paul."

"Then you could tell her how brave her great-great-great-great granddaddy and mammy were; how they swum ashore from the wrecked galleon in a raging storm."

"We'll tell her that, Paul."

"Gee willikers," Grandpa's voice cracked, "git agoin' afore we changes our minds and hauls Misty back out."

Mr. Van Meter nodded. He signaled to the pilot to start up the engines. Then he and Mr. Jacobs stepped inside the plane.

"And be careful," bellowed Grandpa above the noise of the engines, " 'bout letting big chunky kids ride Misty too soon. Recomember she's a young 'un yet."

The plane nosed the wind and roared along the narrow spit of land, the sound of its engines deepening as it climbed. It passed over a lone, wind-crippled pine tree, then up and up and out across the channel, away into the blue distance.

"She's over the White Hill!" shouted Paul into the wave of silence that broke over them.

They watched until the plane was swallowed in a white cloud of mist.

"Now ain't that just like a storybook?" Grandpa crowed, while he rubbed the bristles in his ear. "When Paul fust seed her she was all tangled up in a skein of mist, and now she leaves in a sudden swirl of it. Don't it ease the pain of her goin'?"

There was no answer. None at all.

"Don't it?" he insisted, pulling his hat down low over his eye. "That is, somewhat?"

Chapter 10

ALL ALONE AT TOM'S COVE

FOR THE space of a few brief moments, the little huddle of those left behind stood rooted. Whether they still heard or only imagined they heard the purring of the plane, no one knew.

Grandpa let out a sigh that seemed to come from his boots. "Hmpf! You folks can stand here a-moonin'," he said at last, "but as fer me, I got to hyper along to the Pony Pennin' Grounds. This be one of my big days. Some of the strangers from over on the main may want to buy a partic'lar pony with a partic'lar markin', and might be I'll have jes' the one fer 'em. Come along, Paul and Maureen."

Paul shook his head. "If you don't care, Grandpa, I don't believe I want to see any ponies today."

Grandma cleared her throat. "Clarence," she said, "I promised the Ladies' Auxiliary to bring some oysters to the Pony Penning Dinner this noon and to fry 'em myself. If you can spare the children, I'd like to have them take the little boat and gather some Tom's Cove oysters for me. I want to be sure they're good and plump and right fresh out of the sea."

Listlessly Paul and Maureen followed Grandma to the house. They put on their high rubber boots. They took the flannel gloves and the baskets she offered.

As they walked to Old Dominion Point, they stared blindly at the familiar sights. The beach was deserted now except for the little white striker birds tippeting along the shore on their red feet. The milling crowds of yesterday were gone. They were at the Pony Penning Grounds.

In silence the boy and the girl climbed in a small boat with an outboard motor. Paul cast off the mooring line. He started the motor. It sputtered and stopped. He tried again. This time it chugged evenly.

They were sculling the waves now, heading across the inlet. Paul looked dead ahead. He saw a fishhawk strike the surface of the water in front of the boat, then rise again with a fish so large he could hardly fly with it. He saw the lighthouse of Assateague, like some giant's dagger stuck in the island to keep it from floating out to sea. A circle of buzzards wheeled low over Tom's Cove, making a racket that could be heard above the beat of the motor. Idly Paul pointed to them.

Maureen nodded. She cupped her hands around her mouth. "Likely something dead. A shark, maybe," she called to him.

"Something's alive, too," he called back. "It's keeping the birds from swoopin' down."

Now they were so close to Tom's Cove they could distinguish the shrill chirring of the hawks and the high whistle of the osprey. Paul's indifference was gone.

"The live thing's a baby colt!" he cried.

He shut off the motor and beached the boat. He made a sun visor out of his hand. And there, not a hundred yards away, standing quiet, was a spindle-legged foal. It had a crooked star on its forehead. And as it stood there with its legs all splayed out, it looked like a tiny wooden carving against a cardboard sea.

Maureen spoke Paul's thoughts. "He's like the little wooden colts Mr. Lester makes for Christmas." Then she looked down at the quiet thing lying in the sand. Her voice fell to a whisper. "It's not a shark that's dead."

"No," said Paul, "it's his mamma."

They started out of the boat, but when the foal heard the *plash-plash* made by their rubber boots, he gallumphed away, fast as his toothpick legs would carry him.

"Don't go after him, Maureen. He's afeared. Stand quiet. Might be he'll come to us."

Paul's plan worked. When no one gave chase, the foal minced to a stop, then turned his wild brown eyes on them. The crooked star on his forehead seemed to widen the space between his eyes. It gave him an expression of startled wonder.

A quiet stillness lay over Tom's Cove. Even the circle of birds had stopped their screaming. Paul and Maureen made no move at all. They stood as still as the wooden stakes that marked the oyster beds.

Cautiously, as a child who has lighted a firecracker comes back to see if it will explode, so the foal came a step toward them. Then another out of wild curiousness, and another. When Paul and Maureen still did not move, he grew bold,

106

dancing closer and closer, asking questions with his pricked ears and repeating them with his small question-mark of a tail.

Paul's laugh of wonderment broke the spell. "Say! He's somethin'! A fiery little horse colt!"

At sound of Paul's voice, the foal took fright and shied so sharply that all four of his feet were off the earth at once. Then he high-tailed it up the beach.

"He's sassy for one so little," Maureen laughed. "How long do you reckon he's been alone?"

"Not long. His mamma 'pears too old to stand the running yesterday. She's got an F branded on her hip—belongs to the fire company."

"What'll we do, Paul?"

"Don't know. I'm a-thinkin'."

"Let's take him back and bottle-feed him."

"'Course we'll take him back! But how do we rope him without a rope? How do we round him up without a horse? And even should we catch him, how do we hold him in the boat? He'll be lively as a jumpin' bean."

Maureen was fumbling in her mind for an idea.

"We got to gentle him quick," Paul said.

"Grandpa says nothing takes the wildness out of a creature like sea water."

"That's it, Maureen! That's it! We'll drive him into the channel. Then we'll swim out and tow him in."

Their eyes fastened on the colt, Paul and Maureen worked off their boots. "You stay on this side of him," Paul whispered excitedly. "I'll circle wide around on the other side. Then we'll close in and drive him into the sea."

The foal's gaze followed Paul as the boy went around him in a wide arc. Now the three creatures were forming the three points of a triangle, the colt at the tip and Paul and Maureen back at equal distances on either side.

Paul stopped, took a deep breath. Then like any roundup man, he gave the signal. His wild screeching whoop tore jagged holes in the morning. Quicker than an echo came Maureen's cry. They both charged the foal, arms waving and voices shouting at the top of their lungs.

The wild creature stood frozen an instant. Then he became a whirling dervish, spinning around and around in an ever-smalling circle. The roaring humans were coming at him from

both sides, closer and closer. With a gallopy little gait he
headed out into the water.

Splashing after him, yelling at him, Paul and Maureen
drove him out beyond his depth.

"He can swim!" gasped Maureen. "Look at him go!"

For a few brief seconds the baby colt headed out into the deep. Paul and Maureen watched his tiny pricked ears and the ripple he stirred, making a little V in the water. Suddenly the ears drooped.

"Oh, Paul! He's done in!"

With long strokes the boy and the girl were swimming toward the foal. He was no longer a wild thing, skittering away from them, no longer a brave little horse colt pointing his nose to the sky. He was a frightened baby, struggling to keep from being sucked under. He wanted to be rescued. Exhausted with thrashing and kicking, he let the human creatures swim near. The girl's hand touched him, held his nose out of water. The boy took a firm hold of his forelock. It was thus that the three of them came swimming back to shore.

"Maureen!" Paul spoke jerkily to get his breath. "I'll hold Lonesome. You get our boots."

Still holding the tiny forelock, he shook the water out of his own ears. The foal shook his head too, fiercely, as if he could match anything Paul did. Paul laughed at him, and strangely enough the colt let out a funny little laugh too, until Tom's Cove was a jubilant echo of human and horse laughs.

Now Paul placed his arms under the foal's belly and lifted him into the boat.

Maureen stood dripping wet, watching. "Don't call him Lonesome," she said. "That's too sad of a name. Let's call him Sea Star."

Paul seemed to be talking to himself as he took Maureen's

112

rubber boots and pillowed the colt's head on them. "Why, that name's exactly right," he said. He burst out laughing again. "An hour ago we didn't want to look at a pony. Now this orphan has wound himself around us just the way sea stars wind themselves around oysters."

"Oysters!" clucked Maureen. "We plumb forgot them."

"Grandma won't mind," Paul said. "Or will she?"

"'Course not. She'll say a new-borned colt without any mamma is a heap more important. But the ladies of the Auxiliary will mind; they're counting on Grandma's oysters."

Paul found an old gunny sack in the boat and began drying off the foal. "Tell you what, Maureen. We'll take turns watching Sea Star. You can watch him first, while I fill my basket. Then it'll be my turn to watch. Besides, the tide's slacking. Soon the oyster rocks'll ebb bare. Oysters'll be thick as pebbles. In no time we can fill our baskets."

The little colt's sides were heaving as he lay in the bottom of the boat. Maureen knelt beside him, two wet creatures side by side. "You're all done in," she whispered as she combed his mane with her fingers. "Why, your mane's nothing but ringlets. It's curly as your tail—even though it's drenched." She laid her head alongside his. "I can hear your breathing," she said. "It sounds like the organ at church before the music comes out. I kind of feel like I'm in church. The blue sky for a dome. White lamb clouds." She leaned over and traced the star on his forehead. "My, how you'll miss your mamma!"

As if he understood, the little fellow bleated. He scrambled to his feet. When the boat swayed, he tried to plant his legs far apart like a sailor's. Then his knees buckled and he was lying on Maureen's boots once more.

In the distance Maureen could see Paul scrambling over the rocks, picking up oysters, quickly throwing them into his basket. Now he was running back, his basket full.

"It's my turn to watch Sea Star," he called out.

Maureen put on Paul's wet boots. They were too big, but she did not mind. She sloshed along in them, singing at the top of her voice.

> *"Periwinkle, periwinkle,*
> *Come blow your horn;*
> *I'll give you a gold ring*
> *For a barrel of corn."*

Paul sat on the edge of the boat, fondling the colt with his eyes. Occasionally he looked out toward Maureen gathering oysters. But he did not really see her. He was busy in his mind, thinking of the firemen's brand on the mare, thinking of the ten dollars he had won in the bronco-busting contest. He was buying the biggest nursing bottle they had in the store uptown. He was buying milk. He was giving Misty's stall to Sea Star. He was . . .

"*Whee-ee-ee-ee-n-n-n!*" Sea Star was drying out. He was hungry. He was crying his hunger to the whole wide world.

Maureen came running back. "My basket's almost full," she panted. "Let's get a-going. Sea Star's got to eat."

Chapter 11

THE LITTLE TYKE

WHEN GRANDMA BEEBE looked out the kitchen window, she dropped the egg whisk in her hand and did not bother to pick it up, even though it was making little rivers of egg yolk on her clean swept floor.

She rushed out the door and stood on the stoop. Her mouth made an "O" in her face as she watched the strange threesome turning in at the gate. Paul and Maureen looked to her as if they had been swimming with their clothes on. And wobbling along behind them on a lead rope made of vine was a tiny brown colt.

117

"We picked your oysters, Grandma," called Paul.

"And we covered 'em all over with seaweed so they'd stay cool," Maureen said, waving a piece of the seaweed.

Grandma did not seem interested in the oysters. She was looking right over their heads, clear over to Assateague, up to the place where the pine trees met the sky. "The burden is all rolled away," she said quite plainly.

Paul and Maureen caught each other's eye in surprise. They had half expected Grandma to look upon Sea Star as another burden. Instead, she seemed glad to see him! She was coming down the steps now, lightly as a girl.

"You been so long gone, children," she said, "I been beset by worriments. Now I know." Her face broadened into a smile. "You found a lone colt. Ain't he beautiful with that white star shining plumb in the center of his forehead?"

"We had to drive him into the sea afore we could catch him," Maureen told her.

"Land sakes!" laughed Grandma. "You not only catched him, you gentled him! Here, hand me those baskets. I'll shuck my oysters while you make the little tyke comfortable."

She took the baskets and disappeared into the house.

Paul carefully lifted Sea Star and carried him into Misty's stall.

"He's so tired," Maureen said, "he's not even whiffing around to get acquainted."

It was so. Sea Star did not poke his nose into the manger nor smell the old dried cob of corn at his feet. He just stood, rocking unsteadily.

Paul was bursting with things to be done. "I'll get fresh water, Maureen, and some of Grandpa's Arab feed mixture, and a bundle of marsh grass. You get milk from the ice chest, and see if Grandma's got a nursing bottle."

Long legs ran excitedly in opposite directions.

"No," Grandma pursed her lips thoughtfully in answer to Maureen's question. "Yours was the last nursing bottle we had need for. I sent it away in the mission barrel."

Maureen waved her arms in despair.

"But that's no never mind," Grandma said quickly. "I got a bottle of bluing here. We'll just rinse that out good, and we'll cut a finger off my white kid gloves for a nipple."

"Oh, Grandma! Not your beautiful gloves Uncle Ralph sent you on Mother's Day?"

"The very ones. I don't wear gloves, anyway, only on a funeral or a wedding. It's lots more important that orphan colt gets some good warm milk inside him. He's all tuckered out."

"He's spunky," Maureen said. "He ran away from us quick as scat."

"You put some milk to heat and stir in a little molasses," Grandma said. "Between whiles I'll make as fine a nursing bottle as ever money would buy."

A truck rattled into the lane and ground to a stop. Grandpa Beebe's booted feet came clumping up the steps and his voice carried ahead of him:

"Oh, they're wild and woolly and full of fleas
And never been curried below the knees..."

"Ida!" he bellowed through the screen door, "the ladies is askin' when ye're comin'. Ain't ye ready?"

Suddenly he caught sight of the bottle. "What in tunket ye two doin'? Don't tell me another grandchild's been left to our doorstep!"

"Why, that's exactly what happened," laughed Maureen. She took Grandpa's hand and pulled him down the steps. "Come quick, Grandpa! My sakes, you're harder to lead than a new-borned colt. Quick, Grandpa! Paul and me—we got the wonderfulest surprise for you."

Grandpa let himself be pulled across the barnyard and into the corral and up to Misty's stall. Then he stopped dead. For a long time he just stood there staring from under his eyebrows as if he had never seen a newborn colt before.

A rapt smile slowly spread over his face. "I'm a billy noodle!" he said softly. "As purty a horse colt as I ever see."

"Ain't he young?" asked Maureen.

Grandpa clapped his hands on his hips and grinned. "That he is! Carries hisself in nice shape, too, fer one so young."

Paul explained. "He belongs to the fire company. His mare was layin' on her broadside, right on the beach at Tom's Cove, Grandpa. Looked to be an old mare, white hairs growing around her eyes. We got ten dollars, Grandpa, and I—we, that is—you reckon the fire company will let the colt go?"

"Dunno, childern," Grandpa answered. "That's not what's important now. What's fust to my mind is, can anybody keep him? 'Tain't easy to raise up a baby colt without any mamma. Will he eat fer ye? Here, let me try that grass, Paul."

120

Gently Grandpa placed a few wisps in the colt's mouth. He tried working Sea Star's muzzle. "Go on, li'l shaver," he

coaxed. "Start a-grindin' with yer baby teeth. First thisaway, then thataway. 'Tain't half so dry when ye get to chawin' on it. And it's got a delicate salt flavor. Yer ancestors thought it was right smart good. Whyn't you jes' keep a-tryin'?"

The kitchen door squeaked open and Grandma's voice called out, "Maur—een! Your milk's warm."

"Coming, Grandma."

Grandpa stopped Maureen with his hand. His clasp was so firm that the fingers left white bands when he took them away. "Maureen, no!" he ordered. "I oncet raised up a colt on a bottle. 'Twas a horse colt, too, just like this one. And by-'n-by I couldn't poke my nose outen the door but what he'd come gallopin' at me, puttin' his hard little hooves on my shoulders, askin' fer his bottle."

"I think that would be cute," Maureen said.

"It *was* cute," Grandpa admitted, "that is, at first it was. I'd laugh at him and play with him, and like as not go back in and warm up some milk fer him and put 'lasses in to make it taste mighty nice.

"But," Grandpa's voice grew stern, "when that colt was comin' on six month, 'twasn't cute any more. He got too sniptious for anything, and he growed so strong that when he put his hooves up to my chest 'twas like bein' flayed by a windmill. Why, if I didn't have something to give him he got ornery. Dreadful ornery. He'd nip and bite and have a reg'lar tantrum." Grandpa sighed. "Never could do a thing with that colt. Had to sell him up to Mount Airy to a dealer who wished he'd never clapped eyes on him."

Maureen said wistfully, "It would have been such fun to feed him, and poor Grandma's cut a finger off her new gloves and fixed up a nice bottle for him."

"Well, you tell yer Grandma ter just sew that finger right

122

back on! We ain't goin' to have no spoiled brat-of-a-colt around here. Our colts got to be nice and good."

Paul bit his knuckle, trying to keep back the hot words. "We're starving him, Grandpa. He'll die!"

"Shucks, Paul, we ain't even give him a chance. He'll be eatin' gusty-like afore sundown. Now here's what we'll do. I'll make a mash outa our Arab mix and leave it in the stall fer him, and he's got this nice salty grass, and a good bed to lie on, and the sea wind fluffin' up his mane."

Grandpa picked up the bucket with the Arab feed mixture in it. "Come," he urged, "you jest snuck away and let him be all by hisself fer a little while. Like as not he'll lay down and have a real refreshin' sleep, and when he wakes up he'll begin mouthin' things and find 'em good! He'll forget he's a baby and get all growed up in a hurry. I've seed it happen time and time again."

"Does it *always* happen that way?" Maureen asked.

Grandpa grew tongue-tied. He stood, absently riffling the Arab mixture between his fingers. "Most always, child," he said at last. "Now it's gettin' on fer dinnertime and I got to take yer Grandma to the Dining Hall. The ladies is a-waitin'." He turned to go. Then came back. "Hurry and change yer wet duds or folks'll think I grandsired a couple mush-rats. Then ye can ride over to the dinner on Watch Eyes and Trinket. We'll leave the little shaver be. By the way, what's his name?"

"Sea Star," said both children at once.

As they closed the stall door, Sea Star sent a high little whinny out after them.

"Ain't that cute?" chuckled Grandpa. "He's a-whinnerin' fer ye already. My, but he'll be glad to see ye when ye come back. Ye're goin' to have a high-mettled horse colt there," he added.

"That is, pervided the fire chief is agreeable to yer deal."

Chapter 12

RISKY DOIN'S

THE SMELL of good things floated out of the Dining Hall—oysters and clams frying, dumplings simmering in vegetable juices, chickens and sweet potatoes roasting. The steaming vapors ran like wisps of smoke past the noses of the people waiting in line. The line moved slowly, like a snake trying to wriggle into a hole too small for it. Paul and Maureen and Grandpa were part of the line. As it crept forward, Grandpa tried to make talk.

"Paul! Maureen! Stop yer worritin' and snuff up!" his voice rolled out strong. "Get a whiff of what I calls perfume. Don't it make ye feel like a coon-hound hot on a scent?"

125

The boy and the girl did not need to answer. People all
around them were following Grandpa's advice—inhaling the
teasing odors in quick little sniffs, laughing and agreeing with
him.

126

Grandma's friend, Mrs. Tilley, stood at the door taking tickets. She greeted the Beebes warmly when they finally reached the entrance. "You three set up to this table right by the door. It'll be cooler and you can see the visitors come in hungry and go out full as punkins."

127

The Dining Hall was a big, low-ceilinged building with an endless number of long tables, covered with the white paper Maureen had tacked on them. But now the white was almost hidden by great serving dishes of golden oyster fritters and clam fritters and crisp chicken and dumpling puffs and bowls of brown bubbling gravy.

Talk seesawed back and forth from one table to another. Home folks from the island and strangers from the mainland were visiting like old friends. They all seemed to be laughing, throwing their heads back, showing strong teeth like colts, or teeth crowned with gold, or toothless gums, but all laughing.

Always, each Pony Penning time, it was the same. People on all sides of them laughing and making fun. But each year for Paul and Maureen there was a colt nagging at their thoughts, stealing their appetites.

A little white-haired man whose cheek pouch was bulging like a chipmunk's leaned across the table to Paul. "I'll trouble you to pass me the chicken and dumplings, Bub." He waggled his head toward the kitchen. "If they're figuring eight pieces and four people to a hen like they useter do," he piped in a thin voice, "I'm goin' to discombobolate their figuring."

Paul passed the chicken and dumplings.

Grandpa tried to lower his voice. "Childern," he smiled in understanding, "jest 'cause somebody ter home is off his feed 'tain't no reason why ye should be off yers. Now let's us dig right in, and when we've slicked our plates clean so's Grandma and the other ladies kin tell we liked their cooking, then we'll hunt up the fire chief and ask him right out plain whether he don't think Sea Star was sent straightaway from heaven to take Misty's place."

Maureen and Paul smiled back at Grandpa. He never seemed to fail them. They bent their heads over their plates and ate. To their surprise the food tasted good. The oysters were so slippery they did not stick in their throats at all. And they drank glass after glass of tea.

"I guess we had Grandma's fritters," Paul said. "Hers are the prettiest brown."

After dinner the fire chief was nowhere to be found in the milling crowd, so Grandpa stepped up to the announcer's stand in the center of the grounds. "I'll thank ye to call out the fire chief's name in that squawker contraption," he said to the announcer.

"Calling the fire chief!" the voice rang out above the noise of the people and the music of the merry-go-round. "Calling the fire chief! He's wanted at the announcer's stand."

This brought the fire chief weaving his way through the crowd. He was nodding to visitors at right and left, and the cane which he carried when he was tired was nowhere in sight.

The people made way for him until he reached the stand. Then Grandpa Beebe stood in his path.

"Was it you wanted me?" the chief asked.

Grandpa nodded.

The chief's eyes crinkled. "Clarence," he said, "ain't this the best crowd we ever had to Pony Penning? Weather's good, too, and everything's running along smooth as honey on a griddle cake."

Paul and Maureen hung a little behind Grandpa. Paul was tying knots in a piece of string, and Maureen stood twiddling her curls in the wrong direction. When the fire chief caught sight of them, he came a step closer and lowered his eyes to theirs.

"I know you two are feeling sad about Misty, but you done a fine thing. Besides, she'll come home swishing her tail behind her—maybe not for a few years—but one day for certain. Chincoteague ponies is like Chincoteague people. Once they gets sand in their shoes they always comes back."

"That ain't what's eatin' 'em, Chief. I'll let 'em tell ye their-selves while I go make arrangements fer shipping one o' my ponies that's goin' all the way to Sandusky, Ohio."

There was a little silence while the fire chief and Paul and Maureen followed Grandpa with their eyes. They watched him tack back and forth in the sea of people like a sailboat, his old battered hat the topgallant sail. When he was lost to view, Paul and Maureen suddenly felt adrift.

The fire chief drew them to a bench away from the crowd and motioned them to sit down, one on each side of him. Then he helped them with a question.

"You folks at the pony sale this morning?"

"No," Paul answered. "We were oystering over to Tom's Cove."

"So?"

"Yes, sir." Paul spoke quickly now. "And lying on the beach was a mare with the brand of the Fire Department on her."

"Was she solid brown, with no white on her at all?"

"Yes, sir."

"Except she was getting white around the eyes," Maureen spoke up.

"Was she a very good mare, Chief?" Paul asked.

"That she was! Raised up frisky colts. A new one each year. Always hers brought the highest prices at the auction." The fire chief's voice had a faraway tone. "Guess she helped buy a lot of equipment for the fire company," he said. "This year she and the Phantom were the only mares who didn't get rounded up. We figured the Phantom was too smart, but we feared for the brown mare."

A slow tear showed at the corner of Maureen's eye. It grew fuller and rounder and finally spilled over.

"Come, come, child. That mare was full of years. She'd had the free and wild life for nigh onto fifteen years. Don't cry about her, honey."

"I'm not. It's her new-borned baby I'm thinking about."

The fire chief was silent for what seemed a long time. "Hmmm," he said at last. "Had a colt, did she?"

"A baby horse colt," Paul answered. "A beauty! All brown except for a white star in the middle of his forehead. His name's Sea Star."

A smile played about the fire chief's lips and his head nodded as if he saw the spindly legged foal standing all alone at Tom's Cove with the sea at his back.

"Sea Star!" he chuckled. "I declare! You young ones pull just the right name out of the hat. How d'you do it?"

"It was Maureen," Paul said. "I was thinking of calling him Lonesome, but that was too sad of a name. Maureen just said his name right out. 'Sea Star' she said, without even thinking."

Paul shoved his toe in the sandy soil until he almost bent it back. "Chief," he said, "will the Fire Department, you think, sell off the little colt? To us?"

The fire chief pinched his lip in thought. He closed his eyes for a minute. "Sometimes," he said, talking more to himself than to Paul and Maureen, "sometimes the whole Department has to be called together so's a matter like this can be laid on the table for discussion."

A little groan escaped Maureen.

"That's the way of it in most cases." He was about to say more, but one of the roundup men came up, his eyes reddened.

"Got my specs knocked off during the ropin' this morning," he said. "Wonder, Chief, if you could do something about the nosepiece. It's broke."

"Lucky you ain't bug-eyed," the fire chief laughed, "or you'd lost more'n your specs. I'll see they're fixed for you."

He turned back to Paul and Maureen, going right on where he had left off. "Then there are times," he said, "when a thing's so clear we'd only be wasting the men's time if we called up a meeting."

"Yes?"

"This, now, is one of those times," the chief said. "A decision's got to be made quick when a pony's too young to fend for itself. By the way, where's Sea Star now?"

"He's in Misty's stall," Maureen said.

"And," Paul looked at the chief gravely, "we've got ten dollars from the bronc-busting contest, because Mr. Van Meter wouldn't take the money to buy carrots for Misty." Paul leaped to his feet as if an idea had just burst in his mind. "Mr. Van Meter said we might need it for something very special, and Sea Star's it!"

There was a waiting silence while the fire chief opened up a roll of peppermints and offered them to Maureen.

Paul clenched his fists in impatience. He made himself look straight into the fire chief's face. "I reckon we'd need lots more than ten dollars," he said bitterly. "That is, if you'd sell him at all."

Again a little whirlpool of silence while the chief absently folded the tinfoil around the peppermints. "Now I view the matter like this," he spoke at last. "It's risky doin's, laying out money for a colt under three months. Mighty risky." He pocketed the peppermints. "No," he said thoughtfully, "the Fire Department wouldn't think of taking a cent over ten dollars for an orphan. I'm sure on it. Besides," he added, "that baby needs you two! Needs you bad."

Paul and Maureen looked at each other. They wanted to thank the fire chief, but the words would not come, not even in a whisper.

Maureen found her voice first. "Oh, Chief . . . !" she gulped, then could say no more. She threw her arms around his sun-creased neck and whispered an unintelligible thank-you in his ear.

Paul reached for one of the chief's hands and shook it hard. Then he slid his hand into the pocket of his jeans and took out the neatly folded ten-dollar bill.

Chapter 13

NO ORNERY COLT FOR US

WHEN PAUL and Maureen returned home they found everything in the stall just as they had left it. The Arab mash untouched. The grass in the manger undisturbed. The water bucket full. And huddled in a corner of his stall, his head hanging low between his knees, Sea Star was sobbing out his lonesomeness in little colt whimpers.

Maureen's face went red and her lips tightened. "We tried Grandpa's way," she exploded. "Now I'm going to fetch that bottle."

"No, you ain't!" a voice behind them spoke sharply. Maureen hardly knew it for Grandpa's voice, and the sharpness hurt because it was so seldom used.

"I've been doctor-man to my hosses since afore you two was borned." A fierce light of pride came into his eyes. "In all my days I raised up only one colt to be mean and ornery, and I promised myself I'd nary do it again. Ye've got to trust me a mite longer. Ye've just got to. Chincoteague ponies is wiry. Tougher than you think."

He stooped down on one knee and looked eye to eye with Sea Star, putting his gnarled fingers underneath the ringlets of the colt's mane.

The colt turned his head and sniffed. Memory told him there was no need to be afraid. He accepted Grandpa and Paul and Maureen as if they were no more nor less than the little wind that sifted in between the chinks in the siding.

Grandpa's eyes were unyielding as he straightened up. "How many Pony Pennings," he asked, "can you two recomember?"

Paul and Maureen thought a moment, counting up on their fingers.

"Seven," Paul said.

Maureen said, "Seven for me, too." Then at a surprised look from Grandpa, she changed her mind, "Well, five for sure, Grandpa."

"All right. Five times ye've *both* seed the wild ponies swimmed across from the island of Assateague to Chincoteague, ain't ye?"

The boy and girl nodded, while Sea Star tucked his forelegs beneath him and lay down on his side. He soon fell asleep to the drumming of Grandpa's voice.

"And five times," the voice went on, "ye've both seed the mares druv into the big pens and the colts cut out and druv into the little pens."

Paul and Maureen nodded again, their eyes watching the foal's sides rise and fall.

"And each time after the cuttin' out was over with, ye've heard the colts bellerin' fer their mammas."

Maureen clapped her hands to her ears as if she could hear the sound now.

Grandpa did not stop. "The youngsters go millin' around in the pens hungerin' and thirstin' and refusin' to tech the water and grasses the firemen pervides. But," and here Grandpa began rubbing the bristles of his ear, "but before the week is out, what *always* happens?"

"The colts are eating nice as you please," smiled Paul.

"That's the right answer, Paul! Now I know you're a hoss-man!"

Maureen slipped her hand inside Grandpa's. "We'll wait, Grandpa, afore we think about that nursing bottle again. Sea Star'll be eating like a stallion by the time the week is over, won't he?"

Friday passed. The crowds trickled out of the Pony Penning Grounds and over the causeway to the mainland.

Saturday came, and the mares and stallions were let out of the big pens and driven back home to the island of the wild things. The few unsold colts were driven back, too. They were older, wiser, able to fend for themselves.

At Pony Ranch, Sea Star dozed the hours away. Unlike the other colts, he seemed to have grown littler, younger.

Saturday night came. Darkness drifted down softly over Chincoteague. The moon rose slowly, unrolling a broad carpet of silver out across the Atlantic.

It found Paul's bed and tickled his face with its beams. He turned to the wall, but the moon would not be put aside. It rode through his sleep. In his dreams he was flying on a moonbeam, lighting a path through the woods for the Phantom, lighting a schoolyard in New York where crowds of children were pressing in on Misty, stroking her neck with grubby fingers. He was lighting a desk in Richmond where Uncle Clarence Lee sat bent over papers and books.

Then suddenly the moonbeam became a silver lance and Sea Star was dancing in the prick of light it made. Now the

silver lance was cutting the grass in wide swaths, showing the colt how tender it was, and soon Sea Star understood. He began ripping it, grinding it with his baby teeth.

Paul awoke. He listened sharply. It was only the wind shaking the pine needles.

He jumped from his bed. He looked out over the flat tongue of land where the silver plane had landed. The moon was still shining brightly. He dressed and quietly opened the door of his room. The guinea hens were beginning to wake. They were clacking loudly. Paul was glad. Now his footsteps would not waken Grandma and Grandpa. He passed their closed door. He came to Maureen's door and almost collided with her. There she was, tiptoeing out into the hall.

"What you fixing to do?" whispered Maureen.

Paul's sheepish grin was lost in the dark. "Sh!" he said, putting his finger to his lips. "I'm going to make a warm gruel."

Maureen's mouth flew open. "Why, that's exactly what I was fixing to do!"

In single file they stepped wide of the boards that creaked and came down into the kitchen. A light glowed brightly over the stove and there was Grandma stirring oatmeal porridge and reading her Sunday school lesson as she stirred.

"Well, I never!" she gasped at the two surprised faces before her. "I thought I was seeing owls. I just got up early to prepare my lesson," she explained. "Come sit down and eat a morsel of porridge. Though I *was* fixing it for someone else—a four-footed critter."

Maureen caught Grandma's hand and clasped it tight between both of hers. "Oh, Grandma," she said, "you're the understandingest grandma in the whole wide world."

Paul fumbled under the sink where the pots and pans were kept. He found an old one that had lost a handle and held it up for Grandma.

She looked at it and nodded. Then she spooned out a big helping of the steaming meal and sprinkled a handful of brown sugar over the top of it.

"Go along, you two. Our breakfast can wait until after you coax Sea Star. Always and always it'll be the same here, I reckon. The ponies comes first, then the people. Go along while I memorize my text." Her words trailed out after them, "'And the angel of the Lord stood among the myrtle trees . . .'"

Chapter 14

THE GENTLEMAN FROM KENTUCKY

SEA STAR refused the porridge.

Maureen said, "He spits it out as if 'twas vinegar."

"He was somethin'!" Paul said. "Just look at him now. Ribs showing like a squeeze box." He turned away, stumbling across the barnyard, and headed for the piney woods.

Maureen followed at a distance. The sun was rising. Long shafts of sunlight slid through the trees, gilding one side, leaving the other black. The piney litter underfoot deadened the sound of their feet. Maureen watched Paul's fists go to his eyes and brush something away with the back of his hand.

"Ain't the cobwebs bothersome this time of morning?" she said, coming up to him.

"Sure are," Paul replied, keeping his face ahead. "For a girl, you're right observing."

"Oh, thank you, Paul. I didn't aim to be a tag-along, but I couldn't bear not to come. I figured you'd be brooding something in your mind."

Paul slowed his steps. "I been brooding all right."

"Sure enough?"

The boy nodded.

"What you decided, Paul?"

Paul's voice began to sound more like his own. There was a wild note of hope in it. "One Pony Penning a gentleman was here all the way from Lexington, Kentucky. And he got to talking manlike to me and Grandpa. He had a big nurse-mare farm."

"A nurse-mare farm?"

"A nurse-mare farm."

"What's that?"

"Quit interrupting, Maureen; I'm trying to figure something out. You just listen."

"All right, I will. But oh, Paul, make it good!"

Paul cuffed the pine branches with his hands as he walked, sending dewdrops flying in every direction. It seemed to ease his feelings and loosen his tongue. "This gentleman," he said, "owned lots of draft mares and jennies, and they most always had young 'uns tagging at their heels. Then when a fine Thoroughbred colt from one of the big racing stables near by lost its mamma, why, then the gentleman would rent out one of his mares and the little Thoroughbred would eat off her. He'd grow big and strong."

"Oh, Paul! It's beautiful!" Maureen heaved a loud sigh.

144

"Now all we got to do is rope a mare over on Assateague and rent her from the Fire Department."

Paul snorted in disgust. "'Taint as easy as that. A wild mare'd kick the living daylights out of an orphan colt. She'd want her own colt back, or none at all. She might even kill another colt."

"What if . . . " Maureen gasped with the wonder of the idea that had come to her. "What if the mare couldn't kick? What if her heel string was cut and she couldn't light out with the other heel?"

Paul let out a low whistle. "Why, she wouldn't have a leg to stand on!"

Maureen was beside herself with excitement. "Let's go right back and . . ."

"Wait!" said Paul. "The man told me and Grandpa lots of other things. He said that if the nurse mare didn't want to adopt a strange colt, she could hold herself all tense-like and the milk just wouldn't come out. And besides, the mare with the cut heel has still got a mighty good set of teeth and she could bite. Bite hard." Paul opened his jaws and snapped them sharply together. The sound sent a shiver through Maureen.

"What we got to do," Paul said, "is to make that mare *want* to take on Sea Star for her very own. *That's* what we go to do."

For several minutes they followed along the winding path in silence.

Maureen slipped past Paul, her bare feet making no noise at all. "Hmpf!" she taunted. "If your man from Kentucky was so awful smart, how did he do it?"

Paul did not answer right away. He kicked a pine cone along the path with his toes until it scuttered behind a tree trunk. He peered into a deserted redbird's nest. "I recomember now!" he said as if he had found the answer among the twigs and rootlets of the nest. "He told us he used to rub the colt all over with sheep dip. Then he'd rub the mare's nose with it, too. He'd trick her into thinking the colt was hers 'cause they smelled the same."

Now the words were tumbling over each other. "He told about a lady stable owner, too, who was in the perfume business, and she rubbed a mare and an orphan colt with the same perfume, and the mare took on the colt."

Maureen halted, nodding to herself as if she had discovered something very wise and secret.

"Paul! Whiff! Like this." She drew the pungent odor of the myrtle trees deep into her lungs, and laughed as she blew it out again. "What smells so good and perfumey as our own myrtle leaves?"

The wind had picked up the fragrance from the thicket of myrtle trees ahead and was blowing it in their faces. Now they both threw back their heads like colts and snuffed it in greedily.

A muffled, rustling sound! A crackling of brush! A sudden stirring in the clump of myrtles!

Startled, Maureen touched Paul's arm and pointed to the swaying branches. They both hung back, motionless, listening. The feathered *whish* of bird wings? The pawing of a wild deer? An otter? Questions went unasked as the sound faded out, then began again.

146

"Might be Grandma's lesson come true," whispered Maureen in awe, "might be the angel of the Lord standing among the myrtle trees."

"It *is!*" shouted Paul. "It's Grandpa Beebe!"

Chapter 15

A HAUNTIN' SMELL O' MYRTLE LEAVES

THERE CAME an answering shout, and a familiar face with white, spiky whiskers peered out of the frame of myrtle leaves. The face rimpled into a sudden smile, and a voice rolled out strong:

"Oh, they're wild and woolly and full of fleas
And never been curried below the knees. . ."

"Childern!" laughed Grandpa. "Ye come just in time to help. I got some empty gunny sacks here and I want 'em filled plum full o' . . ."

"Myrtle leaves!" cried Paul and Maureen in the same breath.

Grandpa nodded in surprise as he gave one sack to Paul and another to Maureen. Then he reached toward a branch, talking as he stripped the leaves. "Once there was a gentleman here from . . ."

"Lexington, Kentucky!" Paul filled in the words, grinning.

Grandpa's head turned around and his eyes went wide. "And this gentleman had a . . ."

"Nurse-mare farm!" Paul and Maureen shouted in unison, like actors in a play.

Both hands suddenly went up to Grandpa's ears and he began rubbing the bristles hard. "I ain't a-pridin' on myself," he chuckled, "but now I know fer sure there's somethin' of the best of me in the both of ye!" His laughter bubbled low, then rang out in the stillness of the woods.

It was good to have work to do. Old gnarled fingers and young smooth ones worked swiftly, stripping off the long narrow leaves, filling the bags.

Grandpa brought out his knife and cut off vines that got in their way. "I couldn't sleep last night for worritin' about that little fella," he said. "Whenever I dropt off, I drempt. I'd be combin' his curly mane with my fingers and feelin' of the little ribs stickin' out like the ribs of Grandma's bumberella. Then right smack out o' nowhere came the man from Kentucky nosin' into my dreams. He tolded all over again how that lady rubbed perfume on a nurse mare and an orphan colt. And next thing I knew, I was sittin' up in bed a-whisperin' to myself,

150

'What in tunket has a more hauntin' smell as our own . . .'"

"Myrtle leaves!" exploded Paul and Maureen.

Grandpa's eyes twinkled. "Yes, sir! There's somethin' in this mental telegraphy all right."

Hands worked faster and faster, filling the bags. Now they were half full.

"Jumpin' mullets! I clean forgot to tell ye who the nurse mare's goin' to be." Grandpa's voice rose and quickened with his fingers. "Last night while the moon was ridin' high, I snuck out the house in my bare feet, horsebacks over to Wilbur Wimbrow's and fetches him out o' bed.

"'Wilbur,' I says to him, 'little Sea Star is bad off. He's gettin' mighty poor. Won't eat. How about puttin' him to the mare that got her heel cut?'"

"What'd he say?" Maureen glanced up, watching Grandpa's face intently.

"Wilbur was never one to mince words. He says to me, 'Clarence, you an' me is 'bout the oldest roundup men we got in Chincoteague, and we both knows mares is notionate critters. They take a notion they don't like a colt and they'll have no truck with it.' Then he minded me of the time we tried to get a mare to be a foster mamma and she jest skinned back her ears and lit out with her heels and like to a-kilt the little stranger."

Maureen gasped.

"But we took a lantern out to the barn and I made sure that the mare was still favorin' her near hind leg. Then I looked at her milk bag and saw 'twas swelled with milk. Wilbur, he followed my glance."

"What'd he say?" Paul asked, scarcely above a whisper.

"He just sort of grunted. Had to admit she wasn't lackin' for milk. 'But will she give it?' he asked.

"Then I told him how we'd smash up some myrtle leaves and

152

souse the colt all over with the oily smell of 'em, and we'd rub the mare's nose with it too, and maybe she'd think 'twas her own colt come back to her."

Paul and Maureen let out a deep sigh.

"Stop, childern!" commanded Grandpa. "We got enough leaves here to souse a whole flock of ponies. Let's git a-goin'."

As they hurried back along the path, Grandpa forgot all about breakfast. He was busy with plans. "Maureen, you bareback over to Wilbur Wimbrow's. He's waitin' to help ye with the mare. Me and Paul will fix up the colt till he smells like a whole clump of myrtle. Then we'll hist him into the truck and bring him to his new mamma."

When Maureen was up on Watch Eyes and had gathered the reins in one hand and taken the bag of myrtle under her arm, Grandpa waited a moment before opening the gate for her. He beckoned Paul over to his side. "If you two was jes' little childern," he spoke to them slowly, thoughtfully, "I wouldn't have you to worry. But bein' as ye're nigh growed up, I got to tell you this idee *might* not work." Then his voice rolled out like a steam calliope. "Git a-goin', child. What's keepin' ye? Are ye glued to the earth?" And he slapped Watch Eyes on the rump.

Maureen spurred him with her heels. "Giddap, Watch Eyes. Faster! Faster! You can help."

Watch Eyes liked the idea. He stretched out as if he were racing his own shadow. It was all Maureen could do to turn him in at Wimbrow's lane. He wanted to go on and on into the morning.

The clatter of hooves brought Mr. Wimbrow out of his house, carrying a steaming pail in one hand and a wooden bowl with a potato masher in the other.

"Morning, Maureen," he said. "Put Watch Eyes in that stall next to the mare."

154

Maureen looked up into the lean, weathered face of the roundup man. She gave him a small nervous smile as she led Watch Eyes to the empty stall.

"I'll need you to grind up the leaves," Mr. Wimbrow said. "Here's our potato masher and a bowl. I was just fixing to bathe the mare's heel. You can sit in the doorway and work. It'll do the mare good to begin getting a whiff of the myrtle."

Maureen pounded and beat the leaves. The fragrance filled her nostrils until it wiped out the smell of the disinfectant Mr. Wimbrow was using.

Her eyes slid over the mare as she worked. She saw how Mr. Wimbrow had tied her to a corner of the stall to keep her from moving about and using the hurt leg. She saw the mare turn her head to watch what was going on. But there was no sharp interest in the way she watched. It was the same look that Sea Star had—a sad, dulled look as if nothing at all mattered.

"This cut ain't healing like it should," Mr. Wimbrow worried aloud, sloshing the water over it with his hand. "Some say we should put ice packs onto it. Some say we'd ought to plunge it in hot salt water. I'm doing the best I know how." He sighed, feeling along the tendon. "But what I think is, she's a-grievin' so she ain't even trying to get well."

He threw the bucket of water out of the door and came back to tie up the heel with a clean bandanna. "Likely it'd be better if you rubbed her nose with the myrtle," he said. "She's still got the wildness in her. She thinks of me as someone who keeps bothering that hurt foot. But you, now," he smiled down at Maureen, "you can be a messenger from the woods, bringing gifts of myrtle."

Maureen's hand trembled a little as she scooped up a mound of crushed leaves and slowly went around to the mare's head. She held out her hand just far enough away so the mare had to reach for it. Suddenly the nostrils began to quiver. That familiar fragrance! It seemed to stir memories of the warm places, deep in the woods; memories of the life-giving myrtle, green when all the grasses were dried. She lipped a taste of it, and as she rolled it on her tongue Maureen rubbed oily fingers around one of the mare's nostrils. At the touch of fingers she drew back snorting, her muscles twitching in fright.

Maureen's heart was thumping wildly now. She waited for the mare's fear to pass, waited seconds before the quivering nose reached out again and she could rub the other nostril.

Back at Pony Ranch every hand was busy. Paul grinding the leaves in Grandma's clam grinder, Grandma sewing bags of cheesecloth, and Grandpa stuffing them with myrtle.

"If anybody'd ever said I'd be sewing on the Sabbath day," Grandma said to herself as her needle flew, "I'd have low'd my head in shame. But here I am, sewing for all I'm worth, and out in a stable against my ruthers. Queer how a young 'un can nudge in and upset all your notions."

"That's the way of it," Grandpa chuckled softly. He nodded his head in Paul's direction. "And don't it beat all how fast Paul's a-grindin'? The sweat's rollin' off him. If 'twas clams, now, instead of myrtle leaves, he'd be cool as a cowcumber and there'd be mighty few clams grinded."

"That's what I admire about Paul," Grandma said with certainty. "When something important's at stake, he pitches in."

A look of understanding shuttled between Paul and Grandma.

All this while Sea Star drowsed in a corner of the stall. The smell of myrtle excited no memories in him. Sometimes he cried in his sleep and woke himself up. Then listlessly he would watch the strange doings of the humans.

"Now, Paul," Grandpa said, "ye can grab a bag of myrtle and rub Star from stem to stern whilst I hold him. Mind ye, don't miss a hair." Putting one hand under the foal's muzzle and grasping his tail with the other, Grandpa lifted him to his feet. "Go to it, Paul. I got him steadied."

Paul began rubbing, timidly at first, then vigorously.

"Why, I believe he likes it," Paul laughed, a little awed, and

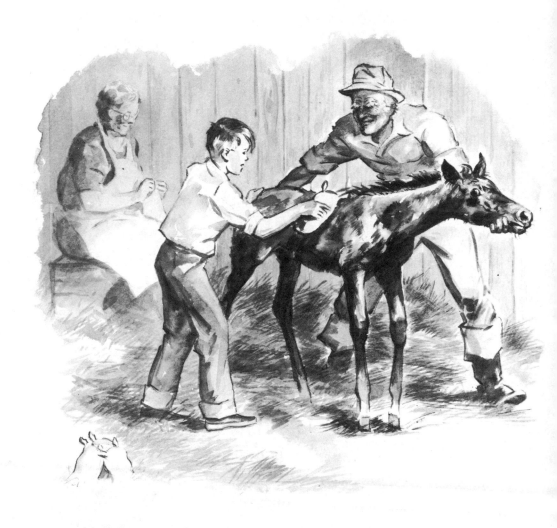

he began asking questions like sparks bursting from a fire. "Does he look more fawn than colt to you? His star, it shines bright on his forehead, see? What makes colts' knees so funny and knobby? Reckon he'll have a left mane like Misty's?"

There was no time for Grandma or Grandpa to answer one question before the next fell.

158

The boy stopped a moment, standing quietly. Then he squatted on his heels and went to work on the foal's face. "Look at me, Sea Star," he said. "When Misty comes back home, you and she can be a team. Misty and Star. Sound pretty to you? And you can run like birds together and you can raise up foals of your own, and Maureen and I can race you both and we won't care which wins. And . . . I guess I need a fresh bag, Grandma. This one's all squinched out."

Occasionally Sea Star fought for his freedom, but it was a weak little fight, as if he knew he had no place to go if he were free.

He let Paul rub his colty whiskers with myrtle. He let him put some of it in his mouth, but he neither chewed nor swallowed it.

"Guess you won't be needing me any more," Grandma said, picking up the clam grinder and her spool of thread. "I'll go in and read over my lesson just once more. Be sure to come back in time to get me to my class," she called over her shoulder.

Grandpa nodded absent-mindedly. Then he buried his nose in Sea Star's coat. "Yep," he sniffed, "if I closed my eyes, I'd think I was right spang in a clump of myrtle. Now, Paul, carry him to the truck. I'll hyper on ahead and let down the ramp."

All during the ride to Wimbrow's, Paul quieted Sea Star with his voice. "You just lean up against me," he said. "Never knew the roads were so bumpity. But I'll stay close to you for comfort. Once I spent a whole night in a truck with Misty. I'd do it for you, too," he breathed into the silky ear.

Chapter 16

LET'S DO SOMETHING

INSIDE WILBUR WIMBROW'S gate Paul set the colt down on the grass. To Paul's surprise, he followed along to the barn as if an invisible lead rope held them together.

Looking at the weak little colt, Mr. Wimbrow shook his head. "Sure is slab-sided," he said. "Let's *do* something!" He turned to Grandpa. "Ought we to blindfold the mare?"

"'Tain't no use. Sea Star's about the color o' her own colt. We'll coax in with him and put him right onto her. Maureen and Paul, you kin look on—if you back up against the wall and stay put."

Matters were out of Paul's and Maureen's hands now. All they could do was to watch the two men wise in the ways of animals.

The stall came alive with expectancy. Mr. Wimbrow tuned his voice down low. He was trying to make it sound natural, but Paul and Maureen felt a tightness in it. "I'll hold the mare's head so she can't turn round and bite," he said. "Clarence, you put the little fellow where he belongs."

He followed his own directions. He took hold of the halter rope close to the mare's chin. He stood there, waiting, without speaking any more.

Grandpa drew in his breath sharply, overcome by the importance of the next few moments. He placed his roughened hand on Sea Star's neck, urging the little fellow forward, inside the doorway of the stall. He turned him gently around, so that Sea Star's nose was at the mare's flanks.

Then he took his hand away.

There was no sound, except for a greenhead fly drumming against a water pail. No one moved. Not the two men nor the boy or girl. The world outside did not exist. There was just a dull, spiritless mare, a weak and hungry foal that did not belong to her, and over all, the pungent fragrance of myrtle oil.

Now the mare filled in the silence. With a sound no bigger than a whisper she began snuffing and blowing and snuffing in again. She tried to turn her head.

Wilbur Wimbrow looked at Grandpa, his eyebrows asking a question.

Grandpa Beebe's head nodded yes.

Mr. Wimbrow let go the rope. The mare could turn her head now. She brought it around slowly toward Sea Star, looking. Now her breathing was quick, as if she had just come in winded from a gallop. And then in the middle of a breath came a quiver of sound. It was like a plucked violin string. It was pain and joy and hunger and thirst all mixed into one trembling note. She and the colt were one! A high neigh of ecstasy escaped her. Fiercely she began licking Sea Star's coat, scolding him tenderly with her tongue all the while.

"My sakes! Look at your coat, will you! Scraggy as anything. No shine to it at all. You been neglected. But I'll make you shining again!" Her tongue strokes said all that and more. She almost upset Sea Star with her mothering. She was shoving him around to suit herself. He was swaying like a blade of grass in the wind.

Paul and Maureen could hardly breathe. Every sound, every motion, seemed sharp and clear. The fly buzzing against the pail, and from some distance away a mocking bird weaving a morning song.

Now Sea Star was questing with his nose, with his lips, moving slowly in toward the mare, drawn in toward her, crying a thin, plaintive mew. Suddenly the crying became a joyous snort—a snort of discovery. He had found the warm bag of milk! He was suckling!

Excitement ran through the stall like flame. Suck! Suck! Grunt and suck! A little brush of a tail flicking back and forth to the rhythm. It said, more plainly than any words, "This is good, good, *good,* I tell you."

For a long time no one spoke. It was enough happiness just to listen to the smothered grunting and to watch the flappety tail. At last Grandpa heaved a great sigh and smiled from one to the other as if they had all come through a great crisis together.

"Jest listen to that little fellow goozle," he said. "That mare gives a lot o' milk, too. Never knew one to take on a colt like that."

"He'll never be no stunted colt now," Mr. Wimbrow said.

"Less'n he drinks so much he'll get stunted carrying it!" laughed Grandpa, relief written on his face.

The mare paid no heed to the voices at all. She had so much to do. Licking and brushing Sea Star's coat to make up for the lost days, and talking all the while in little nickers.

Paul swallowed two or three times before he could make his voice sound like his own. "Sea Star's having his Pony Penning dinner today," he said shakily.

Maureen nodded happily, "And didn't that mare have sharp smellers? She put me in mind of Grandma."

Grandpa caught his breath at mention of Grandma. He squared his hat on his head. "We got to get on, Wilbur. Ida's a great one for gettin' to her Sunday school class on time." He took a final look at the mare. "Most always ye got to watch a nurse mare and an orphan for two-three days afore ye can leave 'em together, but the way she's chattin' over little personal matters with him . . . well, he ain't no lost star now."

Mr. Wimbrow nodded. "Soon as I think the mare can hobble along on her own power, I'll lead 'em both over to Pony

164

Ranch. The children can keep her until Sea Star grows up."

Paul walked out of the stall alongside Mr. Wimbrow. "We'll be glad to pay rent for her like the big racing stables do," he said. "'Course, we can't pay so much."

Mr. Wimbrow roughed his hand over Paul's head. "Really should be the other way around," he said. "The colt saved the mare's life. He come just in the nick of time. She's got something to get well for now."

Chapter 17

OPEN THE GATE

GRANDMA WAS under the pine trees, stirring something in an iron kettle over a fire. She seemed neither ready to go to church nor ready to stay at home. She was wearing her Sunday hat, and over her Sunday dress she had tied a big apron. The smell of chicken steaming with wild onions curled out of the pot. As Grandpa's truck drove in she stopped stirring and waited for the family to come to her.

"You don't need to tell me," she cried. "It's *good* news! Paul's hair is rumpled as a kingfisher's topknot, Grandpa's wearing his hat backside to, and Maureen's been twisting her curls the wrong way. You don't need to let out a peep," she said with shining eyes. "Sea Star's eating! Now we're going to

167

eat, too. We're going to have us a real old-timey Pony Penning feast. You know, you forgot all about breakfast."

Paul and Maureen laughed. They *had* forgotten about breakfast.

Grandpa rubbed his stomach and smacked his lips in pleased anticipation. "To me it smells like outdoor pot pie, simmerin' full of goodness."

"Might be," Grandma said.

Maureen looked into the pot and began stirring. "But, Grandma, what about your Sunday school class?"

"The Lord understood, and so did Mrs. Tilley. She's going to substitute teach for me."

"Ida!" Grandpa scolded in mock sternness, "I never thought I'd live to see the day when you'd get high-toney on yer own family."

"High-toney?"

"Yep, high-toney. Seems to me that when ye wears yer best hat to a outdoor picnic . . ."

Grandma threw her apron over her face and laughed until the tears came. And soon the whole pine grove echoed with laughter.

"Here, Maureen, lay my hat in on my bed. Then you can take the biscuits out of the oven and dish up the Seven Top turnip greens. Clarence, you and Paul slick up. Oh, I haven't been so happy in a week! I've got a hungry family again."

When the picnic table was set and the plates heaped with the chicken pot pie and greens and hot biscuits, they all sat down, Grandpa and Grandma on one bench, Paul and Maureen on the other. Hungry as they were, they did not eat at once. They turned to Grandma, waiting for a word from her.

Grandpa's voice boomed his loudest to hide his real feelings. "Ida, I reckon ye can say grace at a picnic jest as well as to any other time."

Grandma stood up at the end of the table. Her eyes began

to twinkle. "I feel like a colt," she admitted almost shyly. "You know how choicy they are when first they begin to eat? You give 'em some grasses, and they go picking out certain ones that seem saltier than the others, and maybe they hunt for a little bunch of lespedeza."

Paul laughed. "That's just the way they do, Grandma."

"Well, so long as you're not my regular Sunday school class, I'm going to pull out wisps of goodness from the Good Book here and there. 'Tain't the formal way to do, I know. But it's mighty satisfying."

Grandma was shy no longer. She looked up beyond the tallest pine tree, right into the deep sky. She waited for the words to form in her mind. Then she sang them out:

" 'The angel of the Lord stood among the myrtle trees.' "

Maureen's and Paul's eyes met and smiled knowingly.

"'And the morning stars sang together, and all the sons of God shouted for joy.'"

Grandpa's hand went up to the bristles in his ears. "Ida," he chortled, "that's a hull sermon of itself! I like 'em short like that. If I could be in your class, don't know but what I'd be first there ever' Sunday. I'd even brave all them womenfolks."

Grandma's face beamed as she ladled chicken gravy over every plate. Then she sat down.

No one had to be urged to eat. Plates, wiped clean with biscuits, came up for second and third helpings.

"A good thing biscuits don't have pits inside 'em," Paul grinned, reaching for another. "Nobody can count how many I've had."

They ate until they could eat no more. And then instead of going off to chores, they stayed a moment as if caught in some spell no one wanted to break.

"This week is embroidered in my heart," Grandma said. "Just think of little Misty sending Clarence Lee to college!"

Grandpa chuckled. "Y'know," he said, "I kin see the diploma hangin' onto the parlor wall already, and writ on it as plain as plain is the name, 'Clarence Lee Beebe, Jr.' And I'm goin' to print out Misty's name alongside it. And that's all I'll ever read on it," he laughed. "College people wastes words."

Paul swung one leg over the picnic bench and faced out to sea. A silence washed over them, a cozy silence, not sad at all. And running through it were the tiniest sounds that made it even cozier. The wind riffling the pine needles and rustling along the grasses. A duckling trying its wings. Guinea hens scratching. And deep in the woods a wren spilling a waterfall of notes.

Grandpa dropped his voice to fit the quiet. "Me and yer Grandma have had a good many head of children," he mused to himself, "but when each one went off to work or to war, we always got a little dread inside us. Lasted for days. But then . . ."

"Then what?" asked Maureen.

"Always somebody was left behind to stay a spell with us. Even when all our childern was growed up and didn't need us, then you two come along and the empty feelin' was gone."

Paul let out a cry, cut off in the middle. He leaped to his feet. "Look!" he yelled. "Look what's coming!"

Maureen whirled around, almost falling off the bench in her haste. Coming into view at the bend of the lane was a tall, lank man leading a splashy brown-and-white mare. The mare limped a little on her near hind foot, and her head kept turning around as she hobbled along. But it was not her foot that worried her. It was a little brown colt nuzzling along beside her.

"Ahoy, Paul! Ahoy, Maureen!" yelled Wilbur Wimbrow. "Come get your colt and mare. I got to go down the bay oysterin' tomorrow. I can't be wastin' my time on these two. They're yours!"

Paul and Maureen flew to meet them.

"You — know — what?" Paul asked, a little breathless as he ran.

"What?" puffed Maureen.

"Sea Star's come to adopt *us!*"

He called to Mr. Wimbrow. "We're coming! We're coming to open the gate!"

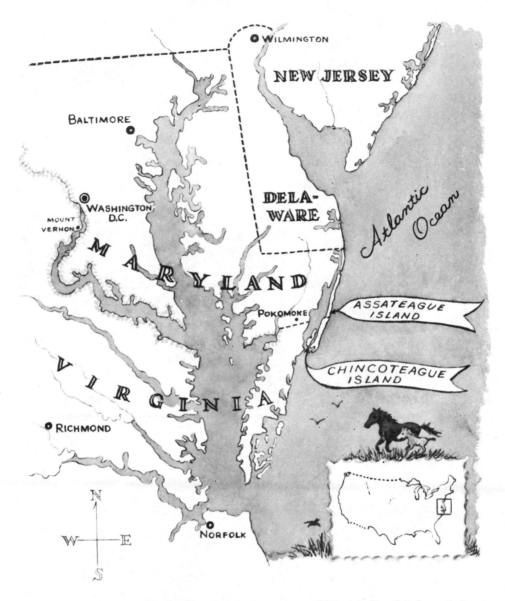

Four miles off the eastern shore of Virginia lies the tiny, wind-rippled isle of Chincoteague. It is only seven miles long and averages but twenty-one inches above the sea.

Assateague Island, however, is thirty-three miles long. Just as Paul Beebe says, Assateague is an outrider, protecting little Chincoteague from the rough seas of the Atlantic. The outer island is a wildlife refuge for wild geese and ducks and the wild ponies.